CLASSROOMS IN CRISIS

PARENTS' RIGHTS AND THE PUBLIC SCHOOL

D1413156

ARNOLD BURRON
JOHN EIDSMOE
DEAN TURNER

ACCENT BOOKS
Denver, Colorado

Scripture quotations marked NASB are from the New American Standard Bible, © The Lockman Foundation 1960, 1962, 1963, 1968, 1971, 1972, 1973, 1975, 1977.

ACCENT BOOKS

A division of Accent Publications, Inc.
12100 West Sixth Avenue
P.O. Box 15337
Denver, Colorado 80215

Library of Congress Catalog Card Number 85-73068

ISBN 0-89636-192-6

Contents

Introduction

Do you identify with Daniel's parents?

Remember Daniel, from the Old Testament? We admire the way he faced death in the lions' den rather than forsake his duty to pray to God. But perhaps you've never thought about his parents.

We don't know their names; they aren't even mentioned in the Bible. But can you imagine how they felt when, after doing their best to raise their son in the Jewish faith, young Daniel was kidnapped by King Nebuchadnezzar and taken captive to Babylon? He was taken to be brainwashed in the Babylonian public schools and trained for a life of civil service in pagan Babylon!

That's where you and Daniel's parents may have something in common. Like them, you have brought children into the world. You have prayed for them, sung to them, read to them, been their example, and done everything you could to raise them in your faith. And then, at an all-too-young age (probably quite a bit younger than Daniel), off they go to public school—not exactly taken captive, but compulsory attendance laws coupled with your own personal financial circumstances sometimes give you little choice in where to send them.

And you wonder. Will my child be safe? Will he learn? Will he be happy there? Most important of all, will he stay true to the Christian principles we have taught him, or will he go the way of the world and forsake his Christian principles and morality? What will school officials do with our child? Will they reinforce the Christian teaching we have given our child or will they undermine it? Is there anything we can do about it?

Yes, your situation is a lot like that of Daniel's parents. But it is different, too. In one way it is worse. Daniel's parents had more time to train him at home. We aren't told exactly how old Daniel was when he was taken to Babylon, but the Hebrew word translated "youths" in Daniel 1:4 normally means young teenagers. In America today, our children usually start public school around age five, and preschool even earlier.

But in other ways your situation is better. Once Daniel was taken captive, his parents could do nothing but pray for him. However, you can do that and more.

You can and should pray for your children. Your children will spend more time in your home than they do in school. You have some control over the public schools in which your child is educated. As a citizen you are part owner of the public schools; as a taxpayer you help pay for them; as a voter you elect the officials who run them. And as a parent you have certain rights concerning your children's education.

What are these rights? How can you assert them effectively without giving needless offense? How can you protect your child's rights and your own rights in a public school setting? How can you work effectively in the public schools to change what is bad and preserve that which is good? After reading this book, it is our hope that you will have a better understanding of your rights concerning the public schools and you will know how to assert your rights more effectively—without jeopardizing the needs of your child.

The authors recognize that the Christian parent will occasionally find himself at odds with public school officials over religion, philosophy, curriculum, or other matters. We believe this book will help you to be listened to with respect when such situations arise.

The authors are not anti-public school. All three were educated in public schools. Two of the authors have been public school teachers; the third is the son of two former public school teachers, the husband of a former public school teacher, and has served as an attorney for several public school districts. Nor are we anti-private school or anti-home school. Two of the authors have sent their children to public schools; the third has chosen home schooling for his children. We believe parents should be allowed to choose from a wide range of educational alternatives. And we believe children should receive a top-quality education regardless of where they attend school. We believe the public schools will function more effectively for all concerned if parents, teachers and administrators know their rights and how to assert them effectively.

So what are your rights? Many readers will approach this book expecting clear-cut answers. In some cases the answers are well-defined; but the day-to-day practice of law often consists of rendering educated guesses as to what the courts are likely to do.

Usually the courts follow past precedents, but on many issues the U.S. Supreme Court has not yet spoken and lower court decisions may be in conflict with one another. Statutes may vary from state to state, and are always subject to change. The fact that a county court in rural New Hampshire decided a case a certain way 50 years ago counts for something; but the Supreme Court of Texas may not feel bound by that precedent today.

We are mindful of the problems of public schools, especially the problem of Christians working within the system. We understand the heartache of Christian parents who believe their children have been alienated from their spiritual heritage by our schools. Studies have shown that among children of church-going families, as many as 80% drop out of church activities during their teen years. The reasons are not entirely clear but it seems likely that schools, with their daily secularizing influence, must bear part of the blame.

Still, we are convinced that Christian parents CAN make a difference! We believe this because we have seen it happen over and over again in numerous exciting examples cited throughout this book.

Remember Daniel's parents? Their prayers were answered. Daniel graduated with top honors from the Babylonian public schools. He performed so well as a Babylonian civil servant that he was made prime minister. And when Babylon fell to the Persians, Daniel continued to serve in the administration of King Darius. Yet, throughout his life of public service, Daniel remained true to the faith of his fathers, refusing to violate the Jewish dietary laws by eating the king's food in the school lunchroom (Daniel 1) and praying faithfully to his God even at the risk of death (chapter 6). Through his testimony and example, Daniel succeeded in bringing King Nebuchadnezzar (chapter 4) and possibly King Darius (chapter 6) to a closer knowledge of God, and God chose Daniel to write the Old Testament book that bears his name.

Daniel excelled in his public schools. There's hope for your child, too!

Chapter 1

Religion And Rights: What Is a Christian Position?

The student from Nigeria patiently answered questions. She had learned to speak English as a child, she explained. She told her fellow graduate students that Nigeria had been a part of the British Commonwealth until 1960. No, Nigeria was not a state in the country of Africa; Africa was a continent, and Nigeria was a country comprised of 19 states with a population of 100,000,000.

After the group had left the after-class conversation session, my Nigerian student confided with the gracious good humor characteristic of her countrymen, how strange it was that Americans knew little about any country except the United States. After a moment of pensive silence, however, the student added this observation: "There is one thing Americans know better than any people on earth," she declared with unequivocal certainty. "Americans know their rights!"

On the surface, this succinct statement appears to be astute— an accurate observation of the awareness of a free people who know their freedoms are grounded in law, and an assessment of the assertive character and indomitable spirit of a people whose very nature is to pursue their rights to life, liberty, and the pursuit of happiness within that law.

But do Americans *really* know their rights? American television exposes millions of viewers to action programs in which police investigations are governed by the Miranda ruling, dictating that even the most repugnant of suspects be advised of his rights. The American media sensationalize the increasingly

9

litigious nature of American society. But the truth is that in some vital areas Americans do *not* know their rights.

For example, most Americans could not answer with any degree of certainty the following True-False questions:

(T=True, F=False, ND=Not Yet Determined)

T F ND   1. The school may spank my child even if I am against using any physical punishment.

T F ND   2. My child can be held back a year in elementary school against my will.

T F ND   3. The school may suspend my child from attending classes as a disciplinary measure, even in elementary school.

T F ND   4. My child can be forced to read a book I object to under threat of failure in the subject.

T F ND   5. I have a right to not allow my child to be assigned to a specific teacher.

T F ND   6. The school may force my child to wear—or not wear—certain clothing.

T F ND   7. I have a right to keep my child home from school, without penalty, for a special occasion including, perhaps, a vacation trip lasting up to ten days.

T F ND   8. I may keep my child out of any class which directly challenges my religious beliefs.

T F ND   9. Teachers may legally present only one side of a controversial issue, such as abortion, to their students.

10

T F ND   10. My child has a right to be included as a member
of the school choir, the school band, or school
athletic teams.

How do you think you did? These questions—and others of
vital importance—will be answered in various parts of this
book.

In the education of our children, an area of vital concern to
parents, Americans do *not* know their rights. As a result, they
often fail to be assertive when they have a right to be. Or they
pick the wrong issue and the wrong time; or the right issue and
time but the wrong adversary.

Ignorance of rights poses numerous problems. Children may
be denied equal opportunity for education. Psychological
damage is sometimes the inadvertent result of well-inten-
tioned, but challengeable, public school practices. Talent may
be overlooked or creatively stifled. Parent-child relationships
are sometimes adversely affected or unique abilities may be
ignored. In short, ignorance of parents' rights in the public
schools can be a serious problem.

Christians, who are to be the salt of the earth and the light of
the world, have a God-given mandate to enhance any situation
in which they find themselves. Their attitudes, behavior,
conduct, and interpersonal relationships are to have an
observable impact on society. They must "salt" the marketplace
of commerce, the marketplace of ideas, and the marketplace of
education.

If Christians are clients of the public schools, their influence
must be persistent, pervasive, and positive. If they are ignorant
of their rights, their influence will be sporadic, bland, and
ineffective—like salt which has lost its savor.

But the problem of Christians and their rights in the public
schools is not only a problem of ignorance. A second problem is
perhaps more complex: Is it appropriate for a Christian to assert
his rights?

The Christian client of the public schools faces these challenges:

1. To learn what his specific rights are in the public schools for the purpose of enhancing his children's education and of influencing both curriculum and teaching methods.

2. To determine the extent to which a Christian can assert his legal rights in a manner consistent with the teachings of Jesus Christ.

When the two challenges are compared, the first challenge is easy to meet. Basic education can equip the Christian with the necessary knowledge to confidently affect his public schools.

The second challenge, however, is not nearly so easily resolved. How does one assert his legal rights in view of these Scriptures?

1. " . . . Do not resist him who is evil; but whoever slaps you on your right cheek, turn to him the other also" (Matthew 5:39, NASB).

2. "And if any one wants to sue you, and take your shirt, let him have your coat also" (Matthew 5:40, NASB).

3. "And whoever shall force you to go one mile, go with him two" (Matthew 5:41, NASB).

4. "Have this attitude in yourselves which was also in Christ Jesus" (Philippians 2:5, NASB).

5. "No soldier in active service entangles himself in the affairs of everyday life, so that he may please the one who enlisted him as a soldier" (II Timothy 2:4, NASB).

6. " . . . Leaving you an example for you to follow in His steps, who committed no sin, nor was any deceit found in his mouth; . . . while suffering, He uttered no threats, but kept entrusting Himself to Him who judges righteously" (I Peter 2:21-23, NASB).

How can the Christian be:

1. assertively humble
2. unyieldingly yielding
3. forcefully meek
4. acquiescently insistent
5. authoritatively non-threatening
6. aggressively conciliatory

In essence, how can a Christian assert his rights in view of the Lord's teachings on humility, meekness, conciliation, service, and non-aggressiveness?

Fortunately, Scripture implies a very clear-cut criterion for selecting which of the behaviors in each of the paradoxical pairs above should be followed. Consider this example from Acts 16:19-40:

The Apostle Paul, along with Silas, is in prison in Philippi. He endures vilification, physical abuse, hardship, and total immobility. His quiet forbearance in suffering and his incredible kindness to the jailer eloquently attest to the truth of the gospel of Christ. The jailer and his whole household receive Christ. At this point, the judges decide to let Paul and Silas go secretly because it seems expedient for them to do so. They send word to Paul that he is free to leave. "Oh no they don't," Paul vigorously asserts. "They have publicly beaten us without trial and jailed us—and we are Roman citizens." Paul then emphatically and boldly asserted his rights, with the result that the judges begged Paul and Silas to leave, no doubt offering their most abject apologies.

The rest of the story is well known. Through Paul's assertion of his rights came the assertion of the gospel of Jesus Christ in Philippi. His initial quiet, humble forbearance was the most appropriate attitude at the time for an effective testimony of the gospel of Jesus Christ. But Paul's subsequent bold, unyielding, aggressively vigorous assertion of his rights was, in that specific situation, just as appropriate.

The standard for Christian action, for selecting an appropriate God-pleasing response in "rights" cases, is the same: That which best honors the Lord Jesus Christ.

If submission, acquiescence, yieldedness and humility best exemplify Christ, then the Christian should gladly relinquish his assertiveness and forego his rights.

If assertiveness, boldness, perseverance, and dogged determination best typify the gospel of Jesus Christ in a Christian, he should unequivocally assert himself and demand his rights.

It is this, then, which must be the guideline for Christians as they determine whether or not to pursue their rights in the public schools.

Chapter 2

Your Rights As a Parent: Where Do They Come From?

Classroom Crisis #1: Early in the 1985-86 school year, a grade school girl in Jenks, Oklahoma—the "buckle" of the Bible belt—passes out salvation tracts to her classmates at school. School officials stop her and tell her this type of activity is prohibited on school property. She and her parents are upset. They see this prohibition as a violation of their rights.

Classroom Crisis #2: Somewhere in the northeast, tenth grader Charles Adan is cut from the football team. Charlie is a good boy, tries hard, and has plenty of spirit. But at 5'2" and 115 pounds he simply lacks the size and strength Central High School needs to win the state championship this year. Charlie doesn't know what to do about the situation, but he feels he has a right to play football and the coach is being unfair.

Classroom Crisis #3: In Los Angeles, Jerry Junkie is suspended from school because a search of his locker reveals three bags of marijuana. He, too, fumes about an invasion of his rights. Whether he smokes marijuana is nobody's business but his, he reasons. Besides, the locker was his private property and no principal had any business opening it.

15

Three situations spanning the country. The first is true, the other two are contrived but could have happened. Each involves entirely different events, but a common thread runs through all. In each situation the student or his parents are concerned about their rights. The child evangelist, the would-be football player, and the marijuana user believe their rights are being violated by school officials.

Not everyone agrees with these conceptions of personal rights. Many contend that Jerry has no right to risk his life and those of others with drugs. Perhaps the coach thinks playing football is a privilege instead of a right, and only the best players qualify. And some may think the grade school evangelist should not pass out tracts on school property because of the separation of church and state.

Americans entertain widely differing ideas of what their rights are and how those rights may be exercised. So, how do we resolve apparent conflicts involving people's rights? How do we know what a person's rights really are in any given situation? And where do we get this notion of human rights, anyway? Is it simply from custom or tradition?

Ultimately, human rights have their source in God. Traditionally, Christians (and many non-Christians) have believed that God is the giver of human rights, that human laws are to conform to God's law, and that human rulers derive their authority from the Supreme Ruler, God.

Sir William Blackstone, who more than any other person was responsible for reducing the common law of England to writing, wrote concerning the divine law which is found in God's Word and the natural law which is dictated by God. He stated that municipal law is man's attempt to apply divine and natural laws to human government, and it is valid only insofar as it corresponds to God's law.

Similarly, Thomas Jefferson wrote in the Declaration of Independence of "the laws of nature and of nature's God." He declared that all men are "endowed by their Creator with certain inalienable rights, that among these rights are life, liberty and the pursuit of happiness." Jefferson clearly recognized God as the source of law and human rights, and he spoke for virtually all of the founders of this nation.

However, in reading through the Bible, you may fail to find a clearly stated declaration of human rights. How then can we claim that human rights come from God? The answer is threefold.

First, human dignity requires a recognition of human rights. Though a fallen creature, man has dignity because he was created in the image of God (Genesis 1:26-27). As the psalmist says, "For thou hast made him a little lower than the angels, and hast crowned him with glory and honour" (Psalm 8:5, KJV). The fact that God has created man in His image and has given him this glory and honor clearly means that man is entitled to certain respect.

It follows logically that violations of human dignity are not appropriate for that which is created in God's image.

Second, the negative commands of Scripture carry by implication a positive affirmation of human rights. For example, the commandment, "You shall not murder," (Exodus 20:13, Romans 13:9) carries an affirmation of the human right to life. The command, "You shall not steal," (Exodus 20:15, Romans 13:9) carries an affirmation of the human right to own and enjoy property.

Third, the delegation of authority from God to man implies a right to use that authority. For example, in Genesis 1:26 we read that God gave man dominion over the fish, fowls and animals of creation. This carries the responsibility to exercise good stewardship (Genesis 2:15) and also the right to use the earth for man's benefit (Genesis 9:3).

How does this apply to education? The Bible places the responsibility for educating children squarely upon parents.

And these words, which I command thee this day, shall be in thine heart. And thou shalt teach them diligently unto thy children ... (Deuteronomy 6:6-7, KJV).

17

The book of Proverbs especially emphasizes the duty of parents to teach their children.

Train up a child in the way he should go: and when he is old, he will not depart from it (Proverbs 22:6, KJV).

Hear, ye children, the instruction of a father, and attend to know understanding (Proverbs 4:1, KJV).

My son, attend unto my wisdom, and bow thine ear to my understanding; that thou mayest regard discretion, and that thy lips may keep knowledge (Proverbs 5:1-2, KJV).

These and many other passages of Scripture place a clear responsibility upon parents to teach their children. In obedience to these commands, the Old Testament Jews faithfully taught their children to read and write, to do arithmetic, to know the history of their people, to be skilled at an occupation, and to know the doctrines of their faith.

Literacy in Old Testament Israel was almost universal among boys and widespread among girls. It had to be because the Jews were the "people of the Book." Jewish children were taught almost entirely in the home until the first century B.C., after which time education remained primarily in the home but was supplemented by the synagogue. Even reading the Torah was part of the religious ritual in the home.

When God gave parents the responsibility of educating their children, He also gave them the right and duty to make sure their children were educated according to His Word.

Since human rights have their source in God, only God can grant these rights. Our government doesn't grant rights; it only secures and protects rights. As Jefferson said in the Declaration of Independence, "to secure these rights, governments are instituted among men."

Our legislature secures rights by implementing statutes, ordinances, administrative regulations and our courts through case precedents. In claiming a right, it is important to know by what authority this right is claimed, and by what means this right is secured. Is it a federal, state, or locally legislated right? Is it in the Constitution, or is it an agency regulation? Is it a court precedent, a local policy, or just a custom or tradition? For example, you would not normally complain to the U.S. Office of Education about a violation of state law. Nor would you complain to the State Department of Education about a violation of local school board policy. You need to know who made the law or policy, whether they had proper authority to do so, and who the proper person or agency is toward which to direct your grievance.

To understand this, let's look at some law-enforcement levels of government.

The United States Constitution

The foundational charter by which authority is delegated to various branches and levels of government is through the United States Constitution. It is the supreme law of the land. The branches of government have no powers that are not expressly delegated or implied through the Constitution. For this reason the Constitution also limits. As the Tenth Amendment states, powers not delegated to the federal government in the Constitution are reserved for the states. It also specifically protects certain rights held by the people. The courts must strike down as unconstitutional any law or policy enacted at the federal, state or local level which is enacted without constitutional authority or which violates personal constitutional rights.

The U.S. Constitution does not delegate education to the federal government. It is therefore fair to assume that the founders intended to leave education to the states and/or the private sector. From the inception of the Constitution (and even before), however, the federal government has taken a *limited* role in education. For example, the Northwest Ordinance of 1787 dividing the Northwest Territories into townships and sections, reserved one section of each township for school use. It was thought that the federal government could do this because the Northwest Territories were not yet states. But the role of the federal government in education has greatly expanded in recent years—in the authors' opinions, far beyond what the founders intended.

Even though the U.S. Constitution does not mention education, certain constitutional rights do apply to our educational system. The Bill of Rights guarantees religious freedom. The First Amendment protects against establishment of religion and against infringement upon free exercise of religion. Other First Amendment protections of free speech, free press, free assembly, and peaceable redress of grievances also apply to some extent to public school students and their parents' rights. The Fourth Amendment protects against unreasonable search and seizure. To the extent this protects the public school student and his locker or desk will be discussed later.

The Fourteenth Amendment guarantee of life, liberty and property has been judged by the courts to include the right of privacy. This right of privacy includes the right of parents to direct and control the upbringing of their children, subject to minimal control by the state. Exactly how much control the state may exercise is still undecided.

The Fourteenth Amendment states, in part, "nor shall any state deprive any person of life, liberty, or property *without due process of law.*" What is due process? United States' courts define the term as elements of procedure which, if omitted, shock the conscience or violate fundamental ideas of fairness. For example, executing a person without a trial or without giving him the opportunity to address the court obviously violates due process. In non-criminal matters such as school disciplinary infractions, some type of hearing may be expected before punishment can be imposed.

The Fourteenth Amendment also provides that no state may "deny to any person within its jurisdiction the equal protection of the laws." It is an overstatement to say that this means the school must treat all students equally. Rather, it means that the schools must not discriminate without having a rational reason for treating someone differently. For example, to give A's to all whites and F's to all blacks solely because of race would clearly violate equal protection. But to award those grades based on academic performance would not violate equal protection because a rational basis exists for this differential.

The Eighth Amendment prohibits "cruel and unusual punishment," but this Amendment does not appear to carry much influence in educational matters.

Recently the Supreme Court addressed a situation in which a junior high school boy was given "more than 20 licks with a paddle while being held over a table in the principal's office." This caused a hematoma which required medical attention and kept him out of school for several days. The sole reason given for the punishment was that he was "slow to respond to his teacher's instructions." Nevertheless, the Court ruled that the Eighth Amendment was intended to apply only to criminal proceedings and not to school disciplinary actions.

The above case did not hold that corporal punishment was justified in that instance, only that it did not violate the Eighth Amendment. It is possible that the parent and child could have pressed criminal assault charges or sued in civil court for assault and battery. An award for this kind of suit was reported by the Associated Press in September 1985.

> An Estes Park [Colorado] student who sued the school district because his principal spanked him has won an out-of-court settlement of $40,000.
>
> [The student], 17, said in his lawsuit he suffered severe bruising when he was paddled as a sixth-grader in 1981 by the Estes Park Middle School principal.... [The student] was paddled for not trying to do his math homework, according to court records.
>
> A jury awarded the boy $40,000 last October but that verdict was overturned and the case was scheduled for a retrial. The settlement was announced on September 13, three days before the retrial was to begin.

When the Constitution was adopted, many argued that a Bill

of Rights was unnecessary because the people already possessed rights under common law, and a government could not repeal those rights except where the Constitution gave the government authority to do so. Alexander Hamilton argued that a Bill of Rights could be dangerous because courts and legislatures could assume that rights not expressly named in the Bill of Rights were forfeited to the state. But others such as Thomas Jefferson and Patrick Henry wanted a Bill of Rights, and to obtain support for the Constitution, a Bill of Rights was promised. To alleviate Hamilton's concern, the Ninth Amendment was included which simply states what most Americans assumed was true anyway: that they retained the rights they had enjoyed under the common law of England and America.

The significance of the Ninth Amendment is that Americans may have certain rights even though they are not expressly mentioned in the Constitution. For example, the courts recognize and respect the right of privacy which includes the right to marry, have children, raise them and educate them without undue interference from the government.

The U.S. Constitution, then, is an important limitation upon government power. Since public schools and school districts are subdivisions of the state, and since teachers and school officials are state employees, they must respect the Constitution. If their actions violate your rights under the Constitution, you have a remedy in court.

Federal Statutes

Federal laws may also limit the authority of school officials and protect parental rights.

Generally, education is viewed as a matter for state, local and private control. However, certain federal statutes do apply to local schools. Since Article VI of the Constitution provides that the Constitution and Laws of the United States shall be the supreme law of the land, federal statutes take precedence over state and local ordinances and even over state constitutional provisions.

For specific information on federal statutes which affect local education consult an attorney. However, some general guidelines on parents' rights follow.

1. The Hatch Amendment gives parents the right to object to certain school practices which violate their religious or moral beliefs.

2. Another statute gives handicapped children the right to certain specialized treatment. Parents whose children are denied this treatment may sue in federal court to require school officials to comply with federal law.

3. A statute in the Civil Rights Act of 1964 authorizes one to sue in federal court if his civil rights, including free speech and freedom of religion, are violated by persons acting under state law. This statute empowers one to sue not only school districts, but also school officials and teachers in their personal capacities, and allows recovery of attorney fees as well as damages.

Federal Regulations

Congress is the only branch of the federal government that can enact legislation. Regulatory agencies are under the executive branch and cannot pass laws; but they can formulate rules and regulations to interpret, administer and enforce the laws passed by Congress. These regulations are legally enforceable but they cannot conflict with congressional legislation.

Most federal regulations which affect local education are issued by the U.S. Department of Education (USDOE), a federal agency that was separated from the U.S. Department of Health, Education and Welfare (HEW) in 1979 to become a cabinet level department in its own right. USDOE regulations are important because, like federal statutes, they often take precedence over local policies and even over state law.

Many USDOE regulations are designed to implement the various civil rights acts and prevent racial, sexual and other forms of discrimination. Some USDOE regulations deal with discrimination in athletics, such as requiring comparable athletic programs for both sexes. Other USDOE regulations govern the use of federal grants. If a school district has received federal funds for certain programs, facilities or equipment, there may be federal regulations which govern who may have access to that equipment or facility, and how it is to be administered.

State Constitutions

Every state constitution contains protections for the rights of its inhabitants. In many states these protections parallel the guarantees of the Bill of Rights, but in some cases they go beyond the Bill of Rights to afford even more protection. Also, even if a state constitutional provision is worded exactly as the federal constitutional provision, it may be interpreted to provide more protection because each state supreme court is considered to be the final arbiter of its own constitution.

Among the important state constitutional provisions are the basic "freedoms"—of religion, of speech, of assembly, of the press. In addition, state constitutional provisions may create local school districts and school boards, and may establish and limit their powers.

State Statutes

In most states the state legislature is given general control over public education. If the legislature directs the State Department of Education to change its policies, generally the Department must comply.

State statutes may protect parents' rights in the public schools in many different ways. Some states have laws which forbid or limit corporal punishment. Others may have statutes which guarantee students the right to a moment of silence, or guarantee religious groups the right of equal access to public facilities. Still others have passed laws which require school districts to allow "release time," during which parents may take their children out of school for a few hours per week for religious instruction. In a few states, laws prohibit assigning homework or scheduling school activities on Wednesday nights to avoid conflicts with church services. Other state statutes may guarantee parents the right to review and object to textbooks or curricula.

State Department of Education Rules

Every state has a Department of Education (DOE) though it may come under different names: Office of Public Instruction, State School Board, et cetera. The executive officer of this department is usually called the State Superintendent. In some states he is an elected official, in others he is appointed. The Department of Education usually has general authority to regulate public education in the state (and in some cases private education, as well), subject to the direction of the legislature and the limitations imposed by the state constitution.

Usually, state regulations will be more comprehensive and specific than state statutes. For example, a state statute may allow public school teachers to use corporal punishment, but the state's DOE regulations may prescribe the manner in which that corporal punishment may take place. If state statutes allow for a moment of silence, the state's Department of Education regulations may detail the time and manner of that moment of silence.

If you believe a state's DOE regulations contradict state statutes (and they sometimes do), you might bring that to the attention of some friendly legislators.

Local School Board Policies

Each school district has a school board; in some states it is called a School Committee or Board of Trustees. The powers of each board should be delineated in state statutes.

Local school board policies must necessarily govern many types of situations: hiring and firing of teachers, discipline of students, student groups, student newspapers, grading, and selection of textbooks. Local school board policies may not contradict state or federal laws but they may define those laws further. For example, even though state statutes and state regulations may allow corporal punishment, local school board policies may prohibit it. However, if state law or state regulation forbids corporal punishment, the local school board may not allow it.

Local School Practices

The local school principal is the executive officer of each local school. He may establish reasonable practices for his school, subject to the rules of the school board, state Department of Education and state law.

Court Decisions

The Constitution, the laws of the United States and of the states themselves cannot address every specific situation. The responsibility for interpreting and applying the Constitution and laws in specific situations rests with the courts.

Court decisions are therefore an important source of school authority and a means by which parental rights are protected. A court's decision that state-written school prayers violate the First Amendment is both a source of frustration for many Christian parents who want their children to pray in school and a source of great protection for others who may object to their children participating in such practices.

Attorney Opinions

Sometimes school policy is based upon an opinion, usually in writing, by the state attorney general or the attorney for the school board. In some jurisdictions this opinion is binding upon the authorities until overturned by a court; in others it is merely advisory and school officials may disregard it. In nearly all instances, school officials will take their attorney's opinion very seriously.

Other Authorities

At times other agencies may exert their authority over the local schools. County commissioners, state and local fire marshals, social service departments, public health officials and zoning agencies all may have rules that affect the public schools. Even city councils may have some authority over local schools. For example, if your city were to pass a tough anti-pornography ordinance, it is doubtful that school textbooks would be exempt.

Uncertainties In the Law

Many who read this will be looking for clearcut answers to all of their questions. Unfortunately, they are likely to be disappointed. In many situations no clearcut answer exists except in the mind of God.

However, it is important that you know the source of your rights and the agencies which protect those rights. When you know the source of a rule, you are in a better position to know how to assert your rights and challenge the rule.

But you may need legal help. How to get it is covered in a later chapter.

Chapter 3

Religious Freedom: Your Rights In Public Schools

"My daughter's teacher told her that Jesus was only a man, not the Son of God, and that He didn't really rise from the dead. That's not what our family believes, and I don't want my daughter to be taught that. What can I do about it?"

A battle for religious liberty is being waged across America today. Nowhere is that battle more intense than in the nation's public schools, for education deals with ideas, as does religion.

One solution to this type of parental dilemma is to simply put up with the objectionable viewpoint while teaching the child the correct doctrine at home. This solution is not totally satisfactory, however. No parent can know everything that is taught in the classroom, so he doesn't always know what to correct.

If your child receives teaching contrary to your beliefs, explain to the child why this concerns you. Be sure your child is not confused about the teacher's statements. You also have the right to talk with the teacher. He may be unaware that his statements might be offensive to some children or parents.

It is important when talking with a teacher to be courteous and non-offensive. All public school teachers are not dedicated, card-carrying secular humanists out to brainwash their students. The majority are simply trying to teach as best they can in order to make a living for themselves and their families. They sincerely want the best for their students, and the cooperation and goodwill of the parents. They may not realize the implications of their teaching or how it might be offensive to Christian parents. A tactful explanation might be very enlightening for teacher and parent alike if the teacher agrees to be more careful in distinguishing fact from opinion or to include alternative viewpoints.

But suppose you and the teacher are at an impasse: he insists he has a right to say what he said, and you insist you don't want your child exposed to that point of view. You need to know where you stand legally. Does the teacher have the right to say what he did?

The First Amendment to the Constitution, properly interpreted, is a sound Biblical concept:

Congress shall make no law respecting an establishment of religion, or prohibiting the free exercise thereof.

Religious matters are beyond the jurisdiction of the federal government. Rightly or wrongly, the Fourteenth Amendment guarantee of "liberty" has been interpreted by the courts to apply the First Amendment to the states as well. Since cities, townships and school districts are subdivisions of states, they, too, are obligated to obey the First Amendment.

The religion clauses of the First Amendment are twofold. The first, "respecting an establishment of religion," prohibits governmental entities from establishing any religious denomination as the official church of the United States or of any political subdivision thereof. But not only is the government prohibited from establishing an official church; it is also barred from taking any action that shows preference for or gives an advantage to one religion over others. One Supreme Court case, *Lemon v. Kurtzman*, established a three-part test to determine whether the government's involvement with religion violates the establishment clause of the First Amendment:

(1) Does the law have a secular purpose?
(2) As its primary effect, does the law advance or inhibit religion?
(3) Does the law excessively entangle the government with religion?

If the law fails any of these tests, the courts must strike it down as unconstitutional.

The second clause of the Amendment "or prohibiting the free exercise thereof," requires government to respect the religious freedom of its citizens. One might say that the establishment clause prohibits the government from establishing any one church, while the free exercise clause means the government cannot prohibit people from attending church.

The free exercise clause protects freedom of belief but it goes further than that. By definition, "exercise of religion" has to be more than religious belief because "exercise" implies action. Free exercise must include not only freedom of belief but also freedom to act on those beliefs.

However, freedom to act is not without limits. If one's actions violate the fundamental rights of other citizens, the state must step in. For example, if my religion calls for human sacrifice, the state will certainly interfere with my free exercise of religion! In another Supreme Court decision (*Wisconsin v. Yoder*), the courts set forth the following three-part test for determining whether the government may interfere with free exercise of religion:

(1) Does the individual or group have a sincere religious belief?

(2) Does the law impose a substantial burden upon the exercise of that belief?

(3) Does the government have a compelling interest (such as health, safety, or national security) that cannot be achieved by any less restrictive means?

In the *Yoder* case, the State of Wisconsin wanted the Amish to comply with the compulsory school attendance law, but they insisted on keeping their children out of formal education after the eighth grade. The Supreme Court recognized the sincerity of the Amish in their religious beliefs and acknowledged that the compulsory attendance law imposed a substantial burden upon those beliefs. The Court further noted that the State has a strong interest in making sure children are educated, so they will be productive, self-supporting citizens, and so they will not be abused in child labor. But the Court found that the State could fulfill its interest without requiring the Amish to send their children to formal schooling; so the Court ruled that the Amish were constitutionally entitled to an exemption from the law.

Perhaps more than any other institution, public schools set the stage for a classic clash between the establishment clause and the free exercise clause of the First Amendment. On one hand, schools are government property, supported with government funds. Compulsory attendance laws provide the public schools with a "captive" audience. And public school teachers and administrators are public officials, paid by government funds. Care must therefore be taken to make sure that what is done on public school property does not run afoul of the establishment clause by enhancing or inhibiting religion or by excessively entangling the government with religion.

On the other hand, public school teachers, administrators and children are citizens, and so are the parents of the children. As citizens they have basic constitutional rights, and as the Supreme Court noted in *Tinker v. Des Moines Independent Community School District*, neither "students nor teachers shed their constitutional rights to the freedom of speech or expression at the schoolhouse gate."

One would think the same is true of the free exercise of religion. Thus, a group of students who want to pray in school may sincerely argue that to deny them the right to meet as a group and pray violates their free exercise of religion. Their opponents might just as sincerely (but wrongly in the authors' opinion) argue that since the school is state property, such activities would violate the establishment clause of the First Amendment.

Christian parents, and those of other religious persuasions, are justifiably concerned that their children learn and accept their religious beliefs and values. They believe their children's happiness, well-being, family harmony, and even eternal salvation may depend upon it. Viewed in this context, it is understandable that they become disturbed when they find that

31

the school system which they support with their tax dollars and to which they have entrusted their children is actually encouraging their children to reject parental beliefs and values.

Most teachers and school officials have no intention of turning students against their parents or causing them to reject their beliefs. But whether it is intentional or not, the Christian parent occasionally finds himself in disagreement with what the schools are teaching his children. The parent who believes in creation may find that the school is teaching evolution. The parent who believes sex outside marriage is a sin against God may find the school is teaching that premarital sex and alternative lifestyles are acceptable. The parent who objects to the occult may find the school's use of witches and goblins at Halloween or the use of games such as Dungeons & Dragons highly objectionable. Other parents may object to pro-abortion teaching, the suggestion that morals and values are relative rather than absolute, and many other concepts which may be opposed to the parents' religious beliefs.

Fortunately, the parent who finds himself at odds with the school system over religious values (or lack thereof) has several legal remedies at his command.

One is the establishment clause of the First Amendment. Courts have interpreted the establishment clause as prohibiting preferential treatment for Christianity or any denomination within Christianity. One must also logically conclude that the establishment clause equally prohibits preferential treatment for non-Christian religions. Furthermore, as we saw earlier, the second prong of the *Lemon v. Kurtzman* test provides that government may not engage in any activity which, as its primary effect, advances *or inhibits* religion. Teaching which has the primary effect of inhibiting Christianity obviously violates this prong of the test.

On this basis, in 1977 a federal district court in New Jersey ruled in favor of a Christian group which objected to the teaching of Transcendental Meditation in public schools on the ground that TM is sufficiently religious in character that its teaching violates the establishment clause (*Malnak v. Yogi*).

In a significant decision, the Supreme Court ruled in a footnote that Secular Humanism is a religion (*Torcaso v. Watkins*). The implications of that ruling in terms of the establishment clause could be very widespread. However, it is necessary to clearly show that the objectionable teaching is closely related to Secular Humanism or that it downgrades one's religious beliefs.

In *Crowley v. Smithsonian*, the Circuit Court of Appeals for the District of Columbia rejected a creationist challenge to exhibits at the Smithsonian Institute which promoted evolution and thereby advanced Secular Humanism. The court reasoned that the mere fact that evolution happens to be compatible with some of the principles of Secular Humanism does not, without more basis, constitute an establishment of Secular Humanism. While the court probably showed a much more tolerant attitude toward Secular Humanism than it would have shown toward Christianity, that is a double standard we will simply have to work with until we can more thoroughly educate the courts.

Secondly, the free exercise clause of the Constitution includes the child's right to practice his religious faith, and the parent's right to teach his religious beliefs and values to his children. When the schools teach concepts which are contrary to the religious beliefs of parents, this imposes a substantial burden upon the parents' exercise of their religious beliefs— especially if the teaching takes place in a dogmatic manner and other positions are not given proper consideration. Certainly a teacher cannot be expected to keep all opinions to himself, for the teacher also has certain First Amendment rights. But there comes a point at which a teacher, as a state employee, must recognize and respect the rights of his students and their parents. When teaching becomes doctrinaire, the teacher has exceeded that point.

Surprisingly, sometimes the free speech clause of the First Amendment is more powerful than the free exercise clause. The courts have ruled that free exercise is violated only when government action imposes a *substantial* burden upon sincere religious convictions. But burdens upon free speech need not be "substantial," and the speech need not be "sincere" to be covered by the free speech clause.

For example, in one case (*Williamsport v. Bender*), students sued the school system when they were denied the right to meet after hours as a student religious group. A federal district court ruled that the prohibition did not violate the free exercise clause since there was no substantial burden. The students were free to meet off-campus. However, the court said, the prohibition against religious groups *does* violate the free speech clause since other student groups are allowed to meet. If the school is open to other groups, officials cannot refuse to allow certain groups simply because the content of their message is religious. A court of appeals overturned the district court speech ruling by a 2-1 vote, and the case is now before the Supreme Court.

Interestingly, the landmark First Amendment case involving the right of religious groups to meet on state college campuses (*Vincent v. Widmar*) was decided on the basis of free speech rather than free exercise of religion.

Closely related is freedom of assembly, the right of students to meet as a group. While the school authorities could probably issue a blanket prohibition against any and all groups meeting on campus, it is questionable whether they can allow some and prohibit others simply because they happen to be religious.

Still another defense is the equal protection clause of the Fourteenth Amendment. This prohibits states from denying any person the equal protection of the law. One might argue that when some students are allowed to assemble and/or express themselves, the equal protection clause requires that Christian students be given the same right.

In any discussion of the religious rights of parents of public school children, several factors must be kept in mind. First, America is in many ways a pluralistic nation. People of many different religious beliefs live here and the First Amendment protects all of them.

For that reason, the First Amendment is a two-edged sword. If, as Christians, we are to enjoy freedom of religious expression, we have to accept the fact that others have freedom of expression also—even to express views we find objectionable. This is true in society as a whole; it is particularly true in the public schools.

It follows that if the public schools are to be open to the Christian viewpoint, they must also be open to other viewpoints as well. And this creates a real dilemma. In recent years Christians have complained that the public schools do not teach values. Yet, if the schools try to teach values that differ from those of orthodox Christians, the complaints become even more strident, and understandably so. The values taught in the public schools cannot be exclusively Christian, because non-Christians are citizens with rights, too. Yet, it is almost impossible to teach many subjects devoid of values, and values are ultimately based upon religion.

Many in America have accepted the notion that the best way to be neutral about religious matters is simply to avoid any mention of God. But when reference to God is left out of public schools and the child goes through a curriculum of seven hours per day, five days per week, nine months of the year without mention of God, the message to the student, intentionally or otherwise, is that God is either nonexistent or not sufficiently important to mention. It also says that truth and knowledge can be compartmentalized into two distinct categories, spiritual and secular. Essentially, this embraces the Secular Humanist view that man is of supreme importance and that God, if He exists at all, is to be relegated to the sidelines. This is not neutrality at all, but rather an establishment of Secular Humanism.

The parent who sends his child to public school will have to accept the fact that his child will be exposed to different ideas and values, some of which he will find highly objectionable. But he need not feel that he is sending his child into a totally hostile environment. God's Word, and God the Holy Spirit who inspired

35

and illumines it, can break through even locked schoolhouse doors to bring His truth to a needy generation. Even the First Amendment and the Supreme Court are no match for Almighty God!

Contrary to what some may think, however, the Supreme Court has not tried to totally expel God from the public schools. In the decision that barred Bible reading as a formal act of worship, the Court added, " . . . the State may not establish a 'religion of secularism' in the sense of actively opposing or showing hostility to religion, thus 'preferring those who believe in no religion over those who do believe' " (*Abington Township v. Schempp*).

Declaring in 1951 that "we are a religious people whose institutions presuppose a divine being," Justice Douglas noted the many ways in which religion and government are intertwined, such as the phrase, "under God" in the Pledge of Allegiance and "In God We Trust" on our coins (*Zorach v. Clausen*).

Unfortunately, many school officials have gone much further than the Supreme Court required in eliminating religious activities from their schools. Sometimes they have accepted one-sided opinions of liberal civil liberties groups as definitive statements of constitutional law. If the American Civil Liberties Union (ACLU) screams about lawsuits while Christians meekly submit, school officials are likely to follow the path of least resistance. Christians need to know their rights under the law, and they need to make it clear that they can and will go to court to defend their religious liberty if necessary.

With that background, what rights do Christians have in the public schools, and what can be done if they are infringed?

Remember the situation at the beginning of this chapter—the student who was told that Jesus was just a man? It is impossible to give a definitive answer as to what a court would decide on the teacher's right to make such a statement. But, as explained, you have a right to talk to the teacher. If your meeting with the teacher is unproductive, you might take the matter up with the principal or a member of the school board. Even if they do not wish to take definitive action, they may talk with the teacher and help him to see your point of view. If all of this is unproductive, you might see a lawyer about taking the matter to court.

In a conflict such as this, though, you must always consider the effect your action may have upon your child. If you intend to keep your child in the public schools, he is going to have to live with the teacher, the principal, and the school system you have complained against. You can combat open forms of discrimination, but subtle and perhaps subconscious reprisals are difficult to prove.

It is also important to remember that you might win a battle but lose the war. You might succeed in stopping a teacher from making statements with which you disagree, but in so doing, you might simply harden that teacher's heart and drive him and others further away from the Lord. Matters such as this must be handled with firmness, but also with love, tact and prayer.

What are some other questions you may have to consider?

The teacher assigned a book for required reading that is filled with profanity and illicit sex. I don't want my kids reading that kind of material. What can I do?

Again, this is an unsettled area of the law. The answer may depend in part upon school policy. In your district, who picks the textbooks and determines reading materials? Is it the teacher? The principal? The school board? Was this particular book approved through the required channels, if there are any required channels?

In the absence of a clear school board policy to the contrary, the teacher usually has considerable discretion to determine study materials. One case even held that a teacher may choose study materials over the school board's objections, so long as the materials chosen were not legally obscene (*Keefe v. Geanakos*).

37

However, allowing a teacher to choose study materials is one thing but allowing that teacher to force his students to read those materials over their or their parents' objections is quite another.

The parent who objects to an assigned book should first meet with the teacher to explain his concern. Emphasize that you are not necessarily saying that the book should be banned, burned or taken out of the library. You are not even saying that the teacher should not assign the book to the class. All you are saying is that you and your child have sincere religious objections to reading the book. Emphasize also that you are not asking to be exempt from the assignment. Rather, express your willingness to have your child read another book of equal or greater length and difficulty which is similarly relevant to the subject matter. Be prepared to suggest an alternative book and be open to alternatives that the teacher may suggest. Affirm that your child is willing to fulfill all the requirements including a report to the class on his book.

While the use of an alternative book seems eminently reasonable and will probably be acceptable in most instances, in a few cases it might not. If going to the principal, superintendent and school board are also unproductive, then you might consider going to court.

If you choose to go to court, you will need to demonstrate the sincerity of your religious convictions. Be prepared to explain in Biblical or simple theological terms, your objections to the material. Your lawyer or pastor might be able to help you articulate these objections.

Be prepared also to show how and why reading the book constitutes a substantial burden upon the exercise of your religious beliefs. Explain why you believe your child's moral character and spiritual development could be corrupted by reading the book. Testimony from your pastor concerning the doctrine of your church on such matters could be helpful here.

It then becomes the responsibility of the school system to

show why they have a compelling interest that cannot be fulfilled by less restrictive means. It is difficult to imagine a successful case being presented that shows an objectionable book as so vitally important that the state's interest cannot be fulfilled by reading any other book. If the state argues that allowing students to read alternative selections would result in extra work for the teacher, or administrative confusion, some courts have ruled that administrative expense and inconvenience alone are insufficient reasons to override fundamental constitutional rights (*Stanley v. Illinois; Cleveland Board of Education v. LaFleur*).

Since there is no precise precedent, however, we cannot say with certainty what a court will decide in such a situation. However, we are strongly of the opinion that a parent who objects to an assigned book and who is willing to have his child read a suitable alternative would ultimately prevail in court. A suggested form is included in chapter eight.

Our school teaches evolution and we believe in special creation. Why can't the teacher at least present both sides of the story?

Good question. Certainly there are two sides to the question of origins with qualified scientists and theologians on each side. That being the case, the two-model approach seems only fair and reasonable.

But the two-model approach has not fared well in the courts thus far. Essentially, the courts' reasoning has been that evolution is "science" while creation is "religion." This is inadequate thinking, though. There is scientific evidence for both viewpoints, and both have profound religious implications.

The dogmatism of the liberal community on this subject is rather surprising. Those who, in almost any other context, would argue fiercely for academic freedom and the need to consider all points of view suddenly come "unglued" at the mention of special creation and zealously strive to make sure the concept of special creation never enters their students' minds.

If the ACLU prevails in its drive to maintain the evolutionist monopoly on public school thought, this will be a blow to genuine academic freedom. But there may be alternatives. One alternative might be a law which requires that when origins are studied, scientific evidence for and against the theory of evolution be presented. At least the students would be made aware of the many scientific flaws in evolutionary thought.

Even though individual states may not require a two-model approach—evolution and creation—they cannot prohibit an individual teacher from presenting both sides of the story. The teacher who presents only evolution may be under the mistaken impression that he is not *allowed* to present creation. But the courts have not gone that far, and we don't think they will.

It may also be that the teacher is unaware of the scientific evidence for creation that exists. Here again, a tactful visit with the teacher or administrators may be very productive. But before making such a visit, make sure you are well informed on the subject, or at least bring someone with you who is. Be prepared also to suggest some good, scientific creationist materials. Some excellent works are listed in the Reference section of this book.

We have heard of teachers who have remarked that they were unaware such evidence existed. Some have been converted to the creationist viewpoint. Others who still believe in evolution agreed that their students deserved to hear both sides. If the teacher is unwilling to present the creationist viewpoint himself, he might allow an outside speaker to come to the class and present the creation model.

Should you fail in your efforts to persuade, you might consider legal action. One parent, Kelly Segraves of the Creation-Science Research Center, objected to the fact that the California public schools dogmatically taught his child evolution and did not expose him to any other viewpoint. Mr.

Segraves took the matter to court. Segraves and the State of California finally agreed to a consent judgment which directed that evolution would be taught only as theory and not as fact. The judgment further directed the California State Board of Education to disseminate a policy statement to that effect to all school boards in the state.

One final thought on this subject: A good and often overlooked way to make sure the creationist viewpoint is available to students is to place creationist materials in school libraries and public libraries.

My child's social studies teacher is always trying to convert the class to his own political viewpoint. He can't do that, can he?

It depends on how he does it. As we noted before, the teacher also has certain First Amendment rights of free speech. He is entitled to express his opinions in class so long as he does not indoctrinate his students in a dogmatic or narrow-minded manner (*James v. Board of Education*).

As a public official, his right to express himself in the classroom must be balanced against your right to direct the upbringing of your children. It is sometimes difficult to know exactly where the balance is; that is the role of the courts.

The balance is more in your favor if the subject matter involves your religious beliefs because then you have the protection of the free exercise clause of the First Amendment as well as the parental rights guaranteed by the Ninth and Fourteenth Amendments. What might seem non-religious to the teacher may, in fact, be highly religious to you. A wide variety of beliefs will be recognized as religious if they are sincere and meaningful to the holder.

For example, abortion to some may be simply a political issue, but to you it may be a religious matter as well—especially if you can demonstrate that your beliefs on the subject are based upon your teaching of the Bible, or that the authorities of your church have spoken definitively on the subject. On many issues such as abortion, giving birth control to minors, homosexual rights, military preparedness, patriotism, or pornography, your legal position is enhanced if you can demonstrate that the school's position offends your religious beliefs.

In some instances a teacher's statements may violate school policy or state law. The laws of most states prohibit advocating illegal activity or action designed to overthrow the government by force or violence. Many may prohibit advocating immorality as well. Nebraska Statute 72-213 declares that, "An informed, loyal, just, and patriotic citizenry is necessary to a strong, stable, just and prosperous America." Accordingly, textbooks must "adequately stress the services of the men who achieved our national independence, established our constitutional government, and preserved our union" so as to "develop a pride and respect for our institutions." Schools must also stress "the benefits and advantages of our form of government and the dangers and fallacies of Nazism, Communism, and similar ideologies." A teacher who openly and flagrantly denigrates the United States and its form of government may violate Nebraska law.

Michigan Statute 15.41507 requires advance parental notification if family planning and/or reproductive health are to be discussed in class. The statute further provides that "clinical abortion shall not be considered a method of family planning, nor shall abortion be taught as a method of reproductive health." A health teacher who advocates abortion might be violating this statute.

I object to my child being forced to go through the whole school day without praying. Can't something be done to let God back into the public schools?

One wonders what the founders of this nation would have thought about recent Supreme Court decisions regarding prayer and Bible reading. They strongly opposed an establishment of religion, at least at the federal level. But the very day after Congress passed the First Amendment and sent it to the states for ratification, that same Congress called upon the President to proclaim a national day of public thanksgiving and prayer. It is difficult to imagine that they would have considered a simple, nondenominational prayer to be an establishment of religion.

In 1962 the U.S. Supreme Court ruled in *Engel v. Vitale* that a state composed nondenominational prayer, to be recited by students on a voluntary basis at the beginning of the school day, violated the establishment clause of the First Amendment. A storm of fury broke loose. Public opinion has overwhelmingly opposed this decision, and legislators have repeatedly attempted to overturn the decision through amendments and other means, but so far the decision stands intact.

More recently, on June 3, 1985, the U.S. Supreme Court decided the *Wallace v. Jaffree* case. The State of Alabama had enacted a law which provided that public schools could set aside a certain time each day for a verbatim reading of the opening prayers of the chaplains of the U.S. House or Senate. The Supreme Court struck this down as an establishment of religion. But the most important portion of the decision concerned silent meditation. Since 1978, Alabama had had a statute on the books which allowed a period of silent meditation in school. In 1981 the "for meditation" phrase was amended to provide, "for meditation or voluntary prayer." The sponsor of the 1981 bill testified that his purpose was to "return voluntary prayer to our public schools." Partially for this reason, the Supreme Court ruled that the 1981 amendment had no secular purpose and its effect was to advance religion, so it struck the voluntary prayer phrase down as unconstitutional. However, the "meditation" portion of the statute was expressly upheld as valid.

The *Jaffree* decision rests upon some shaky reasoning, in part because it places too much emphasis upon statements of legislators. And the *Engel* decision goes beyond what the framers of the First Amendment ever intended. But the practical effect of these decisions is not as devastating as some have been led to believe.

First, the *Engel* decision does not prohibit *all* prayer in the public schools. It simply prohibits the state from composing or selecting prayers for student use. By extension, it would probably prohibit a school board from doing the same, and it would probably prohibit a teacher as a state employee from leading his class in prayer. But it does not prohibit a student or teacher from praying on his own. A student or teacher who wishes to do so would almost undoubtedly be protected by the free exercise clause, so long as he does not disrupt the class in doing so.

Second, the *Jaffree* decision allows a period of silent meditation. In some ways this might be preferable to spoken prayer because during silent meditation the child can pray as his parents and pastors have taught him to pray. In our opinion, the *Jaffree* decision does not declare all silent meditation statutes unconstitutional. Rather, the decision simply struck down a later amendment that had a clear religious purpose. Legislatures and school boards often refer to a "minute of silence" without further elaboration.

Unfortunately, some have interpreted both decisions as going much further than they really did. Instances have surfaced in which school children were told by teachers that they could not engage in silent prayer before eating lunch or say a rosary on the school bus. Such brazen examples of religious oppression clearly violate the free exercise clause and have no basis whatsoever in previous court decisions.

Sometimes changes can be effected by educating public school officials about the true meaning of the Constitution. In 1984 the Washington Chapter of the American Civil Liberties Union filed a 122 page petition with the Washington State Superintendent of Public Instruction alleging that certain religious practices in the Washington public schools violate the

First Amendment and demanding that policies be established by which these religious practices would be curtailed.

At first it seemed that the State was going to accept the ACLU's interpretation as though it were fact. But then a group of Christian attorneys known as the Bill of Rights Legal Foundation arranged for the preparation of a detailed response to the ACLU's petition which took a very different position from the ACLU interpretation. As a result, the ACLU's petition was placed on hold and both positions are being given further consideration.

Once again, most public school officials are not hostile to religion or Christianity. If you can show them that the Constitution and the law are on your side, they are likely to accommodate you.

The school bus driver wouldn't let my child on the bus because he was wearing a cross around his neck and carrying a Bible. Doesn't my son have a right to do that?

Almost certainly he does. In 1969 the Supreme Court heard a case involving a high school student who wore a black armband to school to protest the Vietnam war. It ruled that the First Amendment protected his right to do so *(Tinker v. Des Moines Independent Community School District)*. The same principle should apply to religious symbols.

In other decisions, the Court has ruled that public officials may not discriminate against certain forms of speech or expression just because they are religious in nature.

Incidentally, the right to wear religious symbols applies to teachers as well, except possibly for full clerical garb which might be construed as an establishment of religion.

Our daughter used to belong to a Bible club at school, but last month the school board decided to ban the Bible

club because it was religious. Other groups still meet at school; what's wrong with a Bible club?

The school board's prohibition probably violates Federal law. The Equal Access Act of 1984, Title VIII of Public Law 98-377, requires that if other groups are allowed to meet on public high school campuses, religious groups must be allowed on the same basis provided they are voluntary and student-led; do not involve school employees as sponsors or participants, and are not regularly attended by non-school persons.

The question involves the classic clash between free exercise rights and establishment clause prohibitions. In the 1981 case of *Widmar v. Vincent*, the Supreme Court ruled that a student religious group called Cornerstone had a right to meet on the campus of the University of Missouri, Kansas City. The Court based its decision primarily upon the free speech clause, holding that since the UMKC had made its campus a public forum by allowing student groups to meet and discuss various matters, it could not deny the same right to Cornerstone simply because the content of Cornerstone's speech is religious.

One might think *Widmar* settles the issue, but it does not. Opponents argue that the state has more reason to ban religious groups from high school campuses than from colleges because, while college students are mature enough to recognize that meeting on state premises does not imply state sponsorship, high school students are more impressionable. They might think that because Youth for Christ meets on school property, the school approves of Youth for Christ.

We may have an answer to this question soon. In 1983 a federal judge in Pennsylvania ruled that a student initiated religious group had the right to meet at a Williamsport high school. The circuit court of appeals reversed this ruling in a 2-1 decision. The case is now before the Supreme Court, and a decision is expected in the near future. The right of student groups to meet on campus, coupled with the constitutionality of the Equal Access Act, hangs in the balance.

The school my daughter attends will not let her witness. Isn't that her constitutional right?

The answer may depend upon the time, place and manner of her witnessing. At certain times and places schools must be considered public forums. In the halls, during lunch, and on the playground, students talk about personal activities, morals, and many other subjects. The free speech clause of the First Amendment protects your daughter's right to talk about what is important to her, even if that happens to be Jesus Christ, so long as she does not create an uncontrollable threat to school order and discipline.

During class it may be different. Your daughter may not interrupt a math lecture to give her personal testimony, but she should be allowed to mention her religion if it is relevant to the subject matter and if general class discussion is allowed. If the subject is origins, she should be allowed to state her creationist beliefs and present her reasons and evidence so long as she does not monopolize class time at the expense of other students.

In a class discussion of abortion or premarital sex, she has a right to state her beliefs and present her reasons even if those reasons come from the Bible. In psychology, history, literature, social studies and many other subjects, her religious beliefs and her relationship with Jesus Christ could be very relevant, and she should have the right to say so. A Christian parent can help his child learn to express herself and tie her Christian faith into the subject matter.

Her right to express herself probably includes the right to give out religious literature—subject to reasonable time, place, and manner restrictions. If the school allows students to give out literature generally, they probably will not bar your daughter from giving out religious literature. Recent cases have argued for the right to receive information or the "right to hear."

The September 23, 1985, issue of *Christian News* reported a case that may turn into a landmark. Students in a Florida sixth grade class were required to give book reports. One girl gave her report on the Bible, declaring that she had chosen that Book "because I believe the Bible is a very important Book which can serve as a guide for daily living."

After the report she gave free copies of the New Testament to classmates who asked for them. During the next class period, however, a teacher confiscated the Bibles, told the girl that giving them out was illegal, and returned them to her. The next day she gave out more Bibles. They were also confiscated, and she was taken to the assistant principal's office, interrogated about her religious beliefs, and told she had "broken the law." The girl pleaded with officials to telephone her mother, but they refused. The Rutherford Institute has filed suit on her behalf in federal district court. If successful, their action could go a long way toward securing freedom of religious expression in public schools.

All of the above discussion should make several points clear. First, "Every prudent man acts with knowledge" (Proverbs 13:16, NASB). Knowledge is important. You need to know your rights, and you need to know what is going on in your child's school.

Second, "A gentle answer turns away wrath" (Proverbs 15:1, NASB). Deal tactfully with public school officials, remembering that you are an ambassador of Jesus Christ (II Corinthians 5:20), and they may judge the Lord based upon what they see in you. Furthermore, if school officials feel your wrath, your child may feel theirs!

Third, "If possible, so far as it depends on you, be at peace with all men" (Romans 12:18, NASB). A lawsuit is a traumatic, expensive procedure that leaves permanent scars on everyone, including the attorneys. Negotiation is almost always preferable to litigation; and many, if not most, public school officials are not hostile to your beliefs. Once they understand your concerns, many will accommodate you if you convince them they can do so legally and without undue cost or inconvenience.

But finally, there comes a time when one must stand up for his beliefs. It may become apparent that no agreement, no compromise, no accommodation is going to be reached. At that point, acting under competent legal advice, it becomes necessary to take action. "Be not ye afraid of them: remember the Lord, which is great and terrible, and fight for your brethren, your sons, and your daughters, your wives and your houses" (Nehemiah 4:14, KJV). Your religious liberty, the rights of your fellow believers, and the moral health and spiritual destiny of your children may depend on it.

Chapter 4

Values In the Schools: Your Rights About What Is Taught and How It Is Taught

Is your child being taught that anything is right if he freely decides that it is?

Has your child viewed a film depicting wife-swapping and cannibalism as part of the social studies curriculum?

Is your child being taught that no values are absolute?

Is your child being taught values clarification?

Do you know what your child is being taught?

Generally speaking, parents know very little about what values are taught in American public schools. From the 1960s to the present, the dominant philosophy governing the teaching of values from the first through the twelfth grades has been Values Clarification. The persons primarily responsible for the development of this philosophy of values education (and the set of techniques for teaching it) are Sidney Simon, Leland Howe, Howard Kirschenbaum, Louis Raths, and Merrill Harmin. In defending their approach to teaching values, Kirschenbaum claimed that about one million persons have attended Values Clarification workshops or have been presented materials on how values should be taught. [1] A bibliography of the primary books and articles written by the above-mentioned authors can be found in the Reference section of this book.

Values Clarification (VC): What Is It?

Since VC has been the only formally and widely adopted method of teaching morality in contemporary public schools, it is essential for parents to understand the basic philosophical assumptions that underlie its purposes. It is important to understand what its claims are; why it is potentially dangerous; why it is so controversial, and what parents can do to prevent their children from becoming its possible victims.

Simply and briefly, the basic presuppositions of values clarification philosophy are:

1. There are no universal or absolute truths (i.e., truths that are true for anybody, anywhere, at any time).

2. There are no universal or absolute values.

3. There are no knowable objective criteria for distinguishing right from wrong, good from evil, humane from inhumane, just from unjust, moral from immoral.

4. All value judgments are purely subjective.

5. Any opinion about right and wrong is as good as any other opinion.

6. There are no intrinsic values (i.e., no values that are in essence better or worse than any other values).

7. People can have moral *beliefs* (we all do), but no one can have any moral *knowledge* (i.e., a certainly reliable way to distinguish true from false, or right from wrong, moral beliefs).

The above seven presuppositions are implicit in all writings produced by the leading proponents of the VC methods of teaching morality. Among professional philosophers of morality, the VC way of thinking about ethical matters is known as *moral relativism*.

Basically, moral relativism denies that we can deal in *truth* as this term is ordinarily defined. Rather, it says that we can deal only in individually different perceptions. If we are to talk in terms of truth at all, then we can say nothing more about it than that it has its focus solely in each individual's purely subjective perception. Literally, this means that there is no reality—no truth—outside of perception. For instance, if nobody on the earth perceived the existence of the earth, then the earth would, in reality, not exist.

According to moral relativism, truth is always changing. It varies from individual to individual. It is nothing more than what each individual personally prefers, or "freely chooses" for it to be. Something is right if the individual freely decides that it is right. It is wrong if he freely decides that it is wrong. There is no ideal that is meant, from the beginning of creation, to ultimately have basic dominion in the world. There are no ideals that apply to all of us alike. Each individual is the sole, ultimate arbiter of all judgments about right and wrong.

Since there are no objective grounds on which to distinguish right from wrong, the teacher must be neutral in all value discussions. He must not teach so-called virtues. He must avoid trying to impress in his students' minds and hearts any particular values or virtues. Since the teacher cannot be certain what experiences any one person will have, he cannot be certain what values or lifestyle would be most suitable for any individual.

In *Values and Teaching*, Raths, Harmin and Simon state that "every individual is entitled to the views that he has and to the values that he holds." They go on to conclude that "by definition and by social right, then, values are personal things." [2]

However, the claim to neutrality is questionable. V.C. teachers instruct students that nothing has value except that which they freely choose. By teaching that there are no absolute values and that all values are equally valid, they espouse moral relativism whether they intend to or not.

Judaic-Christian Values and Basic Needs

Traditionally, Judaic-Christian concepts have held to the conviction that *all* human beings share some intrinsic life needs in common. Also, these concepts maintain that there is intrinsic value in every human being's life, and that our intrinsic needs can be fulfilled only by life's intrinsic values. For example, good health is intrinsically better than bad health. No one wants to be unhealthy. Bad health is never something that is worth cultivating as an end in itself. In other words, in a society of enlightened people everybody would *know* that he ought to recognize and honor the need for good health in himself and in all others. Thus good health is intrinsically valuable because we all have an innate need for it, and one is morally entitled to it insofar as he recognizes and honors the needs and rights of others.

There are several needs which are intrinsic to human nature, and which all human beings possess in common whether or not they are aware of them. Some of these needs are:

(1) the need to love and be loved;

(2) the need for positive self-esteem;

(3) the need for self-discipline, for a sense of accountability for one's decisions and acts;

(4) the need for a sense of personal, permanent accomplishment;

(5) the need for a basic sense of security, a feeling of well-being;

(6) the need for emotional and intellectual integrity (a sense of inner order, a unity of being);

(7) the need for freedom of self-expression, self-realization and growth in one's self-value;

(8) the need for intrinsically valuable knowledge (those things that are *always* worth knowing);

(9) the need for constructive creativity;

(10) the need for the ability to communicate constructively, both with oneself and others;

(11) the need for an appreciation of nature;

(12) the need for a sense of priorities;

(13) the need for faith that existence makes sense;

(14) the need for faith in the conservation of values;

(15) the need for beauty;

(16) the need for hope;

(17) the need for a compassionate and constructive sense of humor and play;

(18) the need for unselfish happiness or joy.[3]

A close examination of values clarification literature reveals that, while its authors deny it in principle, they continually appeal to these needs.

The concepts of intrinsic life needs and intrinsic life values cannot be separated from each other meaningfully. Likewise, the concept of rights cannot be meaningfully separated from the concept of needs and values.

Life's intrinsic values are those that, ideally, ought to be adopted and cherished by everyone, for everyone. For example, unselfish love is love that is as sensitive to the needs and rights of others as it is to its own; unselfish joy— joy that has regard for the joy of others, that does not cause needless joylessness in the lives of others; integrity— wholeness of being, inner harmony, coherence in one's values, perspectives, attitudes, desires and acts; basic security—a feeling of gladness, safety, at-homeness in one's relationship with oneself, others and the world.

These values are not universally understood, cherished and acted upon. If they were, we would live in an ideal world and there would be no need for education in morality or the psychology of human nature. But there are certain moral ideals which all of us ought to have the opportunity to learn about. And once we learn them, all of us ought to act freely to conform to them for the sake of the mutual fulfillment of our lives, out of love for one another and God.

It is as essential to have objective standards in the discipline of ethics as it is to have such standards in the disciplines of physics, chemistry, biology and mathematics. There could be no science of physics without a natural order of invariant truths about the make-up of the physical world. Nor can anyone talk intelligently about moral right and wrong without presupposing that there are *knowable* objective criteria for distinguishing enlightened from unenlightened ways of relating with oneself and others.

There have to be some objective standards which cannot

be reduced to custom. Many customs are brutal and wrong. There must be standards which cannot be reduced to personal preference and taste. Without such objective standards, all judgments about right and wrong would be purely capricious and meaningless. Without some facts, some moral certainty, it would follow logically that there is no binding duty, no ideals that either could or should call for allegiance and commitment.

The advocates of values clarification have shown notorious ignorance of the most basic requirements for a sound philosophy of teaching morality in the schools. In a brilliant, critical article entitled "Something Clarified, Nothing of Value," Dwight Boyd and Deanne Bogden pointedly observed that the VC method of teaching ethics "aggrandizes the trivial while trivializing morality into mere matters of taste." [4]

What Values Can the School Teach That Cannot Be Reasonably Challenged?

There are certain moral ideals which have an objective validity in principle that transcends all the changing fads, fashions, mores, and customs of all societies and generations. The following, for example, are ideals which will hold up under all logical and factual analysis and cannot be reduced to the subjectivity of individual perception, biased opinion, or preference and taste.

1. No one has the right to inflict needless harm and suffering on either himself or others. Value distinctions between morally justifiable and unjustifiable kinds of suffering can be made only by the individual who understands the objective facts about his needs and the needs of others.

2. The individual should be self-reflective, should judge himself cautiously and critically, and should judge others by the same criteria with which he judges himself under identical circumstances.

3. Every individual has the right to freedom of independent and creative thinking and acting, the right to be different as long as he recognizes and honors this same right in all others, and as long as, in his differences, he does not cause needless harm or suffering for either himself or others. God cherishes variety. He created and loves individuality in His children.

4. Every individual has the right to expect responsible recognition of his needs, and to act freely to fulfill his needs as long as he recognizes and honors this same right in all others.

5. Every individual should see himself as an end in himself, rather than as a means to some other person's selfish ends; and likewise, should see all others as ends in themselves, rather than as means to his own selfish ends.

6. Every individual has the right to defend himself from injustice or tyranny, and the duty to do so insofar as he is capable.

7. Every individual has the duty to act to fulfill himself insofar as he is capable, and to fully utilize his capacity to help others fulfill their lives also.

8. The individual should seek that alternative to act which will bring the greatest amount of need fulfillment and the least amount of need frustration into life as a whole on a long range basis.

The difficulty of accurately assessing one's own real needs and the needs of others sometimes is very trying, and under complex circumstances may seem to be impossible. But the problematic nature of fulfilling these needs in practice does not alter the fact that they are real needs. Likewise, the problematic nature of fulfilling these ideals in practice does not undermine their validity in principle, nor alter the fact that they are binding. Rather, it simply obligates us inescapably with the duty to continue seeking after more successful means of implementing them.

What's Wrong With Values Clarification?

A careful reading of the literature advocating VC bears out the fact that it appeals unconsciously to the above ideals while theoretically denying that they are possible. For a thorough documentation of this fact, the reader may consult the excellent scholarly work of Kathleen Gow, *Yes, Virginia, There Is Right and Wrong*. This sophisticated, well-documented book clearly reveals what values are being taught in our public schools.

The purpose of VC is not to teach specific facts or truths about how human beings ought to conduct their lives. Rather, the purpose is merely to help the student clarify his values, not teach him how to distinguish between justifiable and unjustifiable values. In *Mein Kampf*, Hitler clarified his values very well. So did Stalin in his various writings. But neither ever succeeded in justifying his motives and efforts to extinguish millions of people.

In *Values and Teaching*, Raths, et al promote the Values Clarification approach. They tell us that the VC teacher is to:

1. Encourage children to make choices and to make them freely.
2. Help them discover and examine available alternatives when faced with choices.
3. Help children to weigh alternatives thoughtfully, reflecting on the consequences of each.
4. Help children to consider what it is that they prize and cherish.
5. Give them opportunities to make public affirmations of their choices.
6. Encourage them to act, behave, and live in accordance with their choices.
7. Help them to examine repeated behavior or patterns in their life. [6]

On first reading, these purposes sound quite sensible. In fact, they are unquestionably techniques that any enlightened teacher of moral values will use with his students. The whole VC system of teaching collapses, however, as soon as one recognizes what is meant by such terms as "help children weigh alternatives thoughtfully."

There is a blatant fallacy in counseling students to "weigh alternatives thoughtfully," while at the same time expressly denying that there are any alternatives that are, in fact, any better or worse to act upon. The Values Clarification system acknowledges no meaningful qualitative distinction between better and worse ways of behaving. VC expressly denies that the teacher should in any way advocate any alternative as better. The VC teacher will never give any reasons why one way of acting is better than another.

Values Clarification reduces the business of making moral decisions to a single criterion, namely the individual's "free choice." What this means, when the face of VC ethics is completely unmasked, is that the individual's free choice is the ultimate standard for any action. Thus, if Idi Amin freely chose to murder thousands of people, it was, in principle, acceptable for him to do so.

However, personal preference, taste and freedom of choice are never reliable criteria for distinguishing between right and wrong. Preferring and freely choosing to do something does not necessarily make it right, any more than preferring and freely choosing *not* to do it necessarily makes it wrong. The indisputability of this fact is borne out in Raths', Harmin's and Simon's own admission that students' choices to steal, cheat and rape in the school are decisions that can never be practically honored.

There is something inherently undignified about a teacher espousing a theory which he himself consistently violates in practice in his classroom. Kathleen Gow focuses attention on this contradiction, indeed hypocrisy, by quoting directly from the second edition of *Values and Teaching:* "What the adult does do is create conditions that aid children in finding values *if* they choose to do so. When operating within this value theory, it is entirely possible that children will choose not to develop values.

It is the teacher's responsibility to support this choice also." [7]

Carrying this to its logical conclusion means that the teacher has no responsibility to help his students learn to understand and respect each other's needs and rights.

Raths, et al continue: "It is not impossible to conceive of someone going through the seven value criteria and deciding that he values intolerance or thievery. What is to be done? Our position is that we *respect* his right to decide upon that value." [8]

Another defender of VC, Clifford E. Knapp, declares decisively that "children are not free to do anything they wish in the society. The first component of the process of valuing is freedom of choice and in some cases society has attempted to restrict personal freedoms through laws for the good of society." [9] Knapp, Raths, et al blatantly contradict themselves. They say that anything is right if the individual freely decides that it is right. But then they add that behavior is not permissible if it interferes with the freedom and rights of others. Thus appealing to certain binding ideals.

Straight down the line, VC purists object to traditional ways of teaching values. They expressly forbid:

1. *Setting an example*, either directly by the way adults behave, or indirectly by pointing to good models in the past or present, such as Washington's honesty or the patience of Ulysses's wife.

2. *Persuading and convincing* by presenting arguments and reasons for this or that set of values and by pointing to the fallacies and the pitfalls of other sets of values.

3. *Limiting choices* by giving children choices only among values "we" accept.

4. *Inspiring* by dramatic or emotional pleas for certain values, often accompanied by models of behavior associated with the value.

5. *Rules and regulations* intended to contain and mold behavior until it is unthinkingly accepted as "right," as through the use

59

of rewards and punishments to reinforce certain behavior.
6. *Cultural or religious dogma* presented as unquestioned wisdom or principle, such as saying that something should be believed because "our people have always done it that way."
7. *Appeals to conscience,* the still, small voice that we assume is in the heart of everyone, with the arousal of feelings of guilt if one's conscience doesn't suggest the "right" way—such as telling a child that he should know better or that he shamed his parents. [10]

At the very core of VC philosophy is the assumption that nothing has any real value except that which is freely chosen. If a teacher inspires his students to want to respect one another, then their feeling of respect has no real value because it is the result of an outsider's influence on their behavior rather than the result of an uninfluenced choice.

Logical Arguments Against Values Clarification

Wise parents want their children to become free, open, and reflective individuals with a strong capacity for self-determination and self-direction. No enlightened parent wants his child to grow into a mindless moral zombie. It is one thing to help children become independent moral and social agents. However, it is an entirely different thing to teach them that being autonomous means having no accountability to any truth about how they ought and ought not to relate with each other.

VC claims to free students from being "apathetic, flighty, uncertain, and inconsistent." It claims also to cure students from being "drifters, overconformists, overdissenters, role-players and underachievers."

There can be no reasonable doubt that some of the procedures used by VC teachers can be helpful in achieving these ideal ends. But unfortunately, there is no evidence that their striking claims have any foundation in fact. On the contrary, there is overwhelming evidence that much time in the classroom has been used inanely, non-productively and even harmfully. While they claim that nothing is certain, at the same time they claim that they can free students from the anxiety of uncertainty.

There have been numerous articles published in scholarly journals by professors who have exposed the many fallacies plaguing VC philosophy and methods. These articles provide substantial argumentation that Values Clarification:

1. *Constitutes a religion,* as religion has been defined by the Supreme Court, and that it violates the principle of separation of church and state;
2. *Is a form of indoctrination,* of an insidious nature because it operates strictly within the framework of rigid relativist dogmas;
3. *Is a violation of the students' right to privacy,* since it queries him, interviews him, and picks his brain about matters that are not the teacher's or the other students' business;
4. *Is pedagogically very narrow* because it excludes other methods, or fails to incorporate other methods, of helping a student learn to distinguish sound from unsound values;
5. *Lacks the support of empirical research;*
6. *Resorts to teaching strategies that can do real psychological damage to some students;*
7. *Violates the civil rights of citizens* who pay taxes financing VC instruction in the schools but do not approve of the values being taught to their children;
8. *Violates the legal requirement of prudence and discretion* by offending many Christian and Jewish students and parents. [11]

In his very meaty article, "The Conflict in Moral Education: An Informal Case Study," Martin Eger provides alarming documentation of how this deeply entrenched ideology at work in the schools has turned children and parents against one another, and divided communities with vehement and vitriolic conflict. [12]

The Life Raft Exercise: What's Wrong With It
The reader should consult Kathleen Gow's book, *Yes, Virginia,*

There Is Right and Wrong, for evidence of how the tactics used in VC can seriously impair some children emotionally rather than enhance their self-image and enthusiasm for life. Special attention should be paid to her discussion of the VC use of teaching strategies.

In one classic values clarification exercise, the "facilitator" (a teacher) has ten students form a circle on the floor. They are then instructed to imagine that they are adrift in a life raft from a boat which sank in a storm. The ten students are told that only nine of them can survive for there simply are not enough supplies to save all of them. One person "must be sacrificed to save the rest." The teacher does not offer the alternative possibility that the ten may choose to die together rather than murder one to save the others.

The facilitator then gives the students thirty minutes to decide who will be the person sacrificed. An alarm clock is set to go off at the end of half an hour. The students are told that unless they have chosen the person to be sacrificed within that time period, the ringing alarm will signify that their raft will have sunk and all will drown. The students are directed by the teachers to make the decision on the basis of democratic consensus. Each student may make a brief case for why he should not be the one sacrificed. Then, a vote is to be conducted and by a majority vote, the group chooses who is to be sacrificed.

The purpose of this "practical strategy" is to help each child decide his own personal worth in relationship to himself and the group. The author of this strategy declares that "the facilitator then directs the group to brainstorm the values that are implicit in the situation they have just experienced." He asks the following questions:

1. What kind of value assumptions did members of the group make?
2. What values motivated the members?
3. What did you learn about your values from an experiential standpoint?

4. In light of this experience, how do you value your own life and the lives of others?
5. What is your worth? [13]

Such a "learning experience" is fraught with danger for the child already suffering from a weak sense of self-worth, and who, under the auspices of his teacher, is chosen to be sacrificed by his peers.

In this case, and in other VC teaching strategies, the criterion for distinguishing right from wrong switches from the individual's personal preference and taste to the group's preference and taste. An analysis of human behavior and history has proven indisputably that neither the individual's choice nor the group's choice is a reliable way of determining right from wrong. The basic relativist assumption implied here is that right and wrong are always a question of who decides.

This method of making moral judgments is entirely too simplistic. In principle, it makes no difference whether a decision is made by a group or by an individual. In either case, once the decision is made the question still arises as to whether it was a right or wrong decision. At this point it is not just an issue of personal preference and taste, but rather an issue of fact. No parent can afford to teach his child that he has the right to do anything that *he* freely decides he has the right to do. Neither can a parent afford to teach his child that he should always go along with decisions made by the group.

Enlightenment can never be reduced to mere perception or opinion be it that of the individual or the group. Values Clarification offers the student no criteria for clarifying his understanding of the truth about his needs and rights or those of others. Neither does it offer him any criterion for distinguishing between justifiable and unjustifiable acts of rebellion against established social mores and laws.

Undoubtedly, some VC teaching techniques can be useful in helping a student develop a stronger identity and an ability to more responsibly shape his own destiny. Whether the general melee of techniques now being used, however, results in more good than harm is being questioned by many thoughtful critics. Some real harm has been done, there is no doubt. To prevent it from happening to their own children, as well as to others, parents can legally do numerous things.

What Can Parents Legally Do To Change Classroom Content or Methods?

They can inquire into their school's policies toward teaching values. Ask the principal, or your child's teachers, whether Values Clarification methods are being used. Listen closely to what your child says about classroom discussions on values. Schools can do only that which they are legally empowered to do by the statutes of the state. If you find that the values being taught in your school are offensive to your religious beliefs and convictions, it is your legal prerogative to complain.

According to the Department of Education regulations, a parent with a complaint must first deliver it to the local school. If the trouble is not settled there, the parent should deliver the complaint to the state education office. If the matter is not settled there, the complaint can be taken to the federal Department of Education. The weakness of this approach is that the Department of Education so far has provided no specific procedures for dealing with complaints on any level. Where such procedures are not clearly provided, the parent should not be surprised if he is subjected to delay after delay with bureaucrats who know no more about what should be done than the helpless parent.

Few parents are aware of their rights as determined by Section 439(a), 1974, in the General Education Act. This Act states:

All material, including teachers' manuals, films, tapes or other supplementary instructional material which will be used in connection with any research or experimental program should be available for inspection by the parents or guardians of the children engaged in such program or project. For the purpose of this section, "research or

64

experimentation program or project" means any applicable program designed to explore or develop new or unproven teaching methods or techniques.

Legally, the school can only foster the teaching of those values that are authorized by its own statutes. Unfortunately, those statutes are generally ambiguous and too broadly stated. For example, "responsible citizenship," "sound values," "intellectual, aesthetic, physical, and moral well-roundedness," "courtesy," "punctuality," "parliamentary etiquette in classroom discussions and public forums" have only *extrinsic* value. That is, they have value only as a means to accomplish good ends, but they can also be used as a means to accomplish bad ends. Courtesy, tact, punctuality, and parliamentary etiquette can be used to manipulate people and to gain power over them.

The VC theoreticians insist that teachers who want to be role models, that those who want to set examples and inspire, are guilty of trying to impose their values on their students. But all teachers teach their personal values one way or another—by what they choose not to talk about as well as what they do talk about. By avoiding the subject of life's intrinsic values, Values Clarification proponents are teaching, in effect, that there are no such values, which is a covert way of indoctrinating students in moral relativism.

What Does the Law Say About Values Clarification?

Not all laws passed through democratic processes are necessarily humane or moral. Some laws are passed merely to meet the selfish aspirations of groups whose vested interests abuse the needs and violate the rights of minorities and individuals, and sometimes even the needs of the majority. It is a mistake to put the authority of the human vote above the authority of those ideals and values that constitute God's will. The Christian must put Christ before any government. He must put Christ before any social institution or system. The "will of the majority" has often been used to rationalize bigotry, chauvinism and racism.

Every state mandates democratic decision-making procedures. It is well known that schools exist to strengthen and propagate democracy. But if this is the only view that is taught, the schools inevitably become instruments of oppression. There is no oppression of the individual as difficult for him to cope with as that which is sanctioned by the 'will of the people' when they are wrong. Enlightened parents must hold the school responsible for teaching ideals and intrinsic life values which will enable its students to fight tyranny—be it that of a dictator, a select few, or the masses.

The only rational way to justify teaching values to a captive audience class is if the teacher is teaching values that are *valuable for everybody in the class*. This means that the teacher is not being paid, for example, to teach middle class, Anglo-Saxon, Protestant values—nor any others that are merely ethnic or racial. The wise teacher knows that he should teach those values that cross all economic, cultural, social, racial and class boundary lines. These must be the intrinsic life values listed at the beginning of this chapter. In teaching these values, the teacher is probably on safe legal, professional and ethical grounds.

The teacher in a tax-supported public school cannot legally indoctrinate a child with values that pressure him to identify with any particular political party or religious dogma (be it theistic or atheistic). This fact is implied unmistakably by the First Amendment to the Constitution which guarantees each individual the right to his own unique ways of thinking—as long as actions based upon those thoughts do not violate the rights of others.

Through the years the Supreme Court has recognized that religious beliefs are inviolable, even though religious practices may be regulated to some extent. The First Amendment embraces two concepts—freedom to believe and freedom to act. The first is absolute but, in the nature of things, the second cannot be.

Your child's right to his beliefs in the classroom "is afforded complete protection under the First Amendment, a proposition accepted consistently and without hesitation by all courts and commentators." [14] No teacher has the freedom to try to change your child's religious beliefs and values if they are harmless to others when acted upon in the school. Likewise, the teacher is free to identify his own religious beliefs and values as long as the manner in which he does it is prudent, discreet and not needlessly offensive to the students or their parents. A teacher cannot digress unduly from teaching the formal subject of his class. He cannot try to indoctrinate impressionable young minds. He cannot attempt to impose his values on students by any form of coercion, subtlety, or subterfuge. Over and over, the courts have passed rulings designed to protect public school children from any encroachment against their right to hold their own religious values.

Without this freedom and these rights, any student is in a cultural and emotional bind because he is constantly treated as an object of pedagogical and environmental conditioning. The character and behavior of the student is programmed into him like that of an android. Our forefathers who designed the Constitution, and those who arranged its Amendments, were admirably sensitive to all oppressors who see those under them as subjects to be manipulated and controlled like robots. While VC preaches against indoctrination of students in any form, it is itself very doctrinaire in its dogmas and methods.

It is essential for Christian parents to realize that the courts have not forbidden only theistic forms of indoctrination of students in the public schools. In *Torcaso v. Watkins*, the Supreme Court classified atheism, agnosticism, Secular Humanism, and other ideologies as *religions*. It is remarkable how many atheists and agnostics erroneously believe that the principle of "separation of church and state" relates only to the propagation of theism, not atheism. On the college level, it is astonishing how many professors feel free to propagandize for atheism in their classes while few Christian professors dare to identify themselves as such.

67

No wise teacher will object to the legal parameters drawn around his academic freedom in the classroom. Likewise, the wise Christian knows that life's intrinsic values can never be forced; unselfish love can never be imposed on anyone. That is a contradiction in terms. Neither can unselfish joy, integrity, dignity, good health or basic security in life ever be forced. A sense of emotional and psychological well-being cannot be imposed. These things come only from the creativity, spontaneity and liberation of the spirit. They are never born of manipulation or coercion.

What Christian Parents Should Not Do

It should never be the purpose of a Christian parent to stifle or prohibit free moral discussion in the public school classroom as some have done. No one need fear the teacher who is trying to teach intrinsic values by example, inspiration, or open and free discussion.

However, when you have certain evidence that a teacher is trying to undermine the values you have taught your child, you can do the following things:

(1) First, you may contact the teacher personally to avoid subjecting him to the threat of needless trouble with his supervisor or principal. This should be done only after careful consideration, however, since your child could become the victim of reprisal if the teacher is closed-minded or unreceptive to your position. It is the responsibility of the supervisor and principal to protect you and your child from such vengeance if the teacher resorts to such unprofessional conduct.

(2) If the private approach is ill-counseled or does not work, you may initiate a teacher-parent-principal conference where you can present the facts that substantiate the violation of your child's rights. If you have no success here, or if you have reason to believe that such a conference is not likely to be productive, then it is your right to confer in private with the principal, or with both him and the superintendent of schools.

(3) If this does not work, you may want to try organizing other

parents who share the same concerns to bring pressure to bear upon the administration. If you have no success there, you have the right to go to the school board.

(4) If no satisfaction is gained by these steps, you may choose to engage the services of a law firm or to take your complaints to the press. The latter alternative is a last resort. It is laden with potentially serious repercussions and should be done only with the greatest care.

Religion Can be Taught in the Schools

In the *Abington Township v. Schempp* case, 1963, the Supreme Court stated that the government cannot establish a religion of secularism, which would be precisely the case if the historical, literary and comparative study of religion were not permitted in public schools. The Court clarified unequivocally that the government cannot adopt a sectarian religious stance showing a preference of any one religion over another. The court opined that "it would be impossible to teach meaningfully many subjects in the social sciences or the humanities without some mention of religion." The Court further contended that "any attempt to impose rigid limits upon the mention of God or references to the Bible in the classsroom would be fraught with dangers." Thus, clearly, the Court recognizes the role of religion in our culture and has never intended to stifle or suppress the expression and discussion of it in the classroom.

In 1984 the Education for Economic Security Act expressly prohibited the use of Federal Magnet School Funds for "any course of instruction the substance of which is Secular Humanism." This clause in the Act reiterates that which was already forbidden by the Supreme Court's ruling in *Torcaso v. Watkins*, the use of tax funds for such purposes. This prohibition, however, was dropped in 1985 when both houses of Congress passed a new version of the magnet-schools program which does not contain the ban.

One other intensely controversial offering in the public school curriculum which was subsidized by federal funds must be mentioned. For years, the most widely consumed set of instructional materials in social studies classes in America has been the teaching package known as *Man, A Course of Studies*. The main reason for its wide use is the fact that its development, advertisement, marketing, and distribution was financed in substantial part by federal funds granted by the National Science Foundation who spent $200,000 to $250,000 yearly "to help promote and market MACOS ... to hold promotion conferences for school decision-makers and officials, to lobby them to buy the program." According to Congressman John B. Conlan, MACOS as a teaching package was rejected by 58 commercial publishers. [15] It is evident that it could never have been successfully published and so widely adopted without the arbitrary use of taxpayers' dollars.

The MACOS film presentation on the Nestilik Eskimo subculture conveys a moral relativist's rationalization of such practices as senilicide, female infanticide, trial marriage, wife-swapping and cannibalism. As could be certainly predicted, thousands of parents complained. In time, the whole teaching package was challenged before the U.S. Congress. Two charges were brought against it.

First, it was charged that the Educational Development Center (which produced it) and the NSF (which heavily financed it) were attempting to impose a uniform, monopolistic social studies curriculum on the nation. They were overriding the need and right of each school district to decide for itself what its schooling needs and instructional materials should be.

Second, they were charged with the misuse of federal funds, infringing upon the rights of private publishers to freedom of competition without government interference. Obviously, no publishing company could provide for the development, advertisement, and lobbying for the sale of an unsaleable product without enormous government subsidies.

Fortunately, the NSF was forced to stop subsidizing MACOS. According to Congressman Conlan, $4.2 million taxpayers' dollars went into the development of this otherwise totally unmarketable educational debacle.

It behooves us as Christians and parents to be vigilant. We must be constantly on guard to keep the academic freedom of our school districts safe from illegitimate intrusions by the federal government, or from ill-considered biases of educators who regard moral relativism as a part of "critical thinking."

A parent should be cautious when considering legal action against a teacher for teaching Secular Humanism in the classroom, though. No action should be initiated unless the evidence is conclusive that the teacher or administrator is trying to stifle the discussion of any theistic religious expressions in the classroom. At this time, not a single case has ever been successfully conducted against a teacher charged with trying to impose Secular Humanism on his students. It is extremely unlikely that any teacher is going to admit that he is a Secular Humanist.

If you have to register a legal complaint, you should charge the teacher with violating the principle of separation of church and state, as interpreted in *Torcaso v. Watkins*, which forbids such behavior.

If you have evidence that the teaching in your child's class is in any way harmful to him or other students, you or your legal representative may appeal to the Hatch Amendment. This Amendment established that federal funds can be withdrawn from any school that imposes unproven experimental teaching techniques on your child. This Amendment is not without its dangers, though. Any experienced educator knows that, in the efforts to improve the quality of teaching, the faculty must be free to experiment with new methods. Wise educators have learned to experiment with new approaches on a pilot basis for the sake of objectivity.

The "Hatch Letter": What's Wrong With It?

The original language of the Hatch Amendment provided that parents must be free to examine classroom curricular materials. But some people have attempted to use the Amendment to prohibit the free discussion of controversial topics which they don't like. A letter distributed by the Maryland Coalition of Concerned Parents on Privacy Rights lists 34 kinds of classroom discussions it considers to be illegal without the express permission of parents. Unfortunately, included in the list are issues of morality, alcohol and drug abuse, suicide, nuclear policy, population control, and witchcraft.

Many Christian educators would object strenuously to so severe a set of restrictions on their freedom of discussion in the classroom. No one should argue that moral discussions should be banned from the classroom. In fact, many students, both Christian and non-Christian, are groping for guidelines. They need some principles on which to peg their daily decisions and they want teachers who can help them discern reality. Many feel aimless and rootless. They don't want teachers who are neutral on all questions. They crave someone who can give them a foundation, help them develop a sense of direction. Moral relativists can give no one a foundation. But without freedom to address the students' questions in a classroom, a teacher cannot offer healing, helpful answers.

One high school teacher remarked, "I'm not at home with the Hatch Amendment as some people interpret it. I'm not that afraid of intellectual liberty in the classroom. Some people, presumptuously in the name of Jesus, would place paranoid limitations on students' and teachers' rights to discuss the great questions of life. How can I help a kid with alcohol and drug problems if we're not free to talk about these things?"

This view probably agrees with that of most Christian teachers in public schools. If such severe restrictions were accepted by the schools, the result would destroy our freedom to discuss those matters which would help students develop thinking minds and a commitment to realistic values. The Maryland Letter, some Christians contend, violates the original spirit of the Hatch Act. It would diminish rather than enhance the possibilities of intellectual and spiritual growth in students.

Sex Education and Other Questionable Curricula

One distinctly quarrelsome area of values education has been that pertaining to sex. Despite the so-called "liberalization era," most Christian parents believe that sexual intercourse is wrong outside of marriage, or if it involves relating with another person as an object. Under no circumstances can a Christian condone moral usury in the selfish manipulation of another person for the sake of sexual pleasure.

Many instructors in sex education courses believe that questions of moral responsibility in sex are too sensitive and disputable to discuss in the classroom. And, of course, the Values Clarification position is that the teacher should remain neutral on any moral questions that might arise. If one looks at all the suffering that results daily from irresponsibility in peoples' sexual lives, one must find such neutrality abhorrent.

Numerous textbooks used in sex education, health, home-making and social studies courses are not neutral on questions of sexual morality. Rather, they espouse sexual permissiveness in a way that is offensive to both Christian and Jewish parents who have a Biblical orientation toward sex. To find certain evidence of this fact, the reader should examine *Humanism in Textbooks: Secular Religion in the Classroom* by Mel and Norma Gabler.

Some states permit courses in sex education and some expressly prohibit them. Overall, the courts have ruled that teachers must use prudence and discretion when discussing sex in the classroom. This means that the teacher should avoid talking about sex in any way that can be reasonably regarded as offensive or vulgar. Generally, the courts have upheld a school's right to offer courses in sex education if they are not prohibited by state statutes and if they are optional for students. Many schools that have adopted such courses have dropped them because of intense parental complaint.

In their book, *Law and Education: Contemporary Issues and Court Decisions*, H.C. Hudgins, Jr. and Richard S. Vacca bring to light an important legal point for parents. In a New Jersey case, the court decided that "a school violated the constitutional rights of students in that it required attendance of children at a course, 'Human Sexuality.' The court held that the course could be offered; however, attendance could not be required. The court noted that if the course teaches a student how to plan a future life and what conduct in life is acceptable, and if these two topics conflict with one's religious beliefs, his free exercise rights [of religion] are violated." [16] Thus a school district probably cannot require your child to attend a sex education course.

Chapter 5

Discipline: What Kinds of Punishment Can Be Used?

In South Lyon, Michigan, a fifteen-year-old high school sophomore was subjected to "an unconsented . . . impromptu shearing of her hair" by her biology teacher, a cheerleading advisor who determined that the student's bangs violated guidelines the teacher had established. The girl's parents filed suit.

A seven-year-old girl in Mesquite, Texas, collapsed and died after running 100 yards as punishment for talking during a physical education class. An autopsy was inconclusive. The superintendent of schools stated that teachers were allowed to discipline students at their discretion and that the teacher would not be disciplined.

Parents of a thirteen-year-old gifted student in suburban Denver, Colorado, filed suit against the school district when their son was forced to sit behind a plywood partition, isolated from his class, because of behavior problems. The isolation, they said, coupled with other educationally unjustifiable teacher behaviors, contributed to their son requiring psychiatric care.

In Worland, Wyoming, a seventeen-year-old senior band student was ordered to the bathroom for refusing to play a solo in class. The student's mother filed suit for damages.

The parent of a high-achieving fifth grader in the Midwest cancelled a long-awaited family vacation trip because of a formally-stated school policy which threatened grade reduction for students who missed school for any reason other than illness or serious family emergencies.

Litigation. Inconvenience. Injudicious disciplinary measures. Physical injury. Emotional trauma. Frustration. Conflicting forces which threaten to abridge the rights of teachers to teach, of students to learn, and of parents to control a vital part of their children's school experience have led to a condition in the public schools which has resulted in extreme reactions by public school administrators and patrons alike in grappling with the problem of discipline.

Chester M. Nolte, an authority in school law who has evaluated cases spanning several years prior to 1980, rendered this startling observation about discipline in the schools: "Principals and teachers are about to run out of effective ways to control and discipline students. Those ways still open are also hedged about with due process and equal protection constraints that make it almost imperative that (a teacher) know what (he) is doing, lest (he) wind up in court."

The problem has spawned extreme measures. In 1984, the Colorado Senate, without debate, voted 33-0 in favor of a bill to give teachers and school officials immunity from lawsuits over student discipline if local codes of school punishment were adopted and then followed. If ever a mandate for parental involvement in policy formulation was apparent, it was apparent in Colorado in 1984. Parents' rights, it seemed, were under assault, and if the action of the Colorado Senate is to become a standard for other states, the rights of the nation's parents are threatened in yet another area of their children's lives. Until extreme measures like the Colorado bill are tested in court, however, past adjudicated cases can be used as a guideline in determining parents' rights. The important point to stress at this juncture is that, as policy making bodies respond to the dual forces of the need for discipline in the schools and of increasing litigation in discipline cases, the opportunity for parents to have an influence in the creation of policy regarding discipline is outstanding.

But what rights do parents and their children have in matters of discipline, particularly in the imposition of the following punishments?

1. Corporal punishment (i.e., spanking)
2. Physical restraint of a child
3. Detention
4. Denial of in-school activities
5. In-school suspension
6. Denial of extracurricular activities
7. Out-of-school suspension
8. Expulsion
9. Academic punishments (i.e., extra work)
10. Lowering of grades
11. In-class isolation
12. Verbal chastening and public criticism
13. Denial of school services (lunch, transportation, etc.)
14. Forced parental involvement
15. Lack of promotion or denial of graduation
16. Reassignment or transfer
17. Search and seizure
18. Humiliation

Parents' rights in each of these areas will be discussed in this chapter. The goal: To enable parents to insist upon the types of discipline best suited for maximum effectiveness in teaching and learning. Only with an appropriate and consistent philosophy of discipline can real progress be made in other reform efforts in the public schools.

Christian parents, armed with a knowledge of their rights regarding discipline, can have a profound influence on the redefining of discipline into a philosophy of "guidance and training," rather than a philosophy of "control and punishment." The formulation and articulation of an appropriate philosophy of discipline seems most likely to be attained with the contributions of well-informed Christians intent on achieving good stewardship in public education.

Basic Principles Christian Parents Should Require

Earlier, it was pointed out that the Values Clarification approach to teaching denies that there are any absolute truths and ideals. In reality, it is impossible for any teacher to maintain even a minimal amount of peace and order, or to give a minimum amount of justice to a student's needs in the classroom without some psychological and moral absolutes. A few of the absolutes inherent in a Christian philosophy of discipline are:

(1) *It is impossible to cure blind hatred with more blind hatred.* No matter how good and respectable the teacher might be, occasionally a student will come into his class and hate him. Some students are predisposed to hate a teacher before they even see him. From past experience with bad teachers and parents, they have acquired a strong negative disposition toward any authority figure. Some students don't feel they need a reason to hate a teacher. They are ready to displace their repressed hostility toward any new authority figure they encounter. When such students address teachers in a hostile tone, a common mistake that teachers make is to respond to hostility with more hostility. This only intensifies the problem for both the teacher and the student.

(2) *The more the student hates the teacher, the more the teacher has to love the student.* The less the student cares about his teacher, and the less he cares to learn what the teacher is trying to teach him, the more the teacher has to feel and show loving care toward him. Care-lessness can be cured only with care. One of the central messages of Christ's teachings is that the care-ful heart can charm the care-less heart.

(3) *It is impossible to cure irrationality with more irrationality.* The more irrational the student is, the more rational the teacher has to be. The more unreasonable the student is, the more reasonable the teacher has to be. Immature students need the ballast and boundaries provided by mature and insightful teachers. The exercise of wisdom and personal self-discipline can effectively defuse and cure undisciplined young people.

(4) *It is impossible to cure impatience with more impatience.* Of course, this does not mean that the teacher has to show unlimited tolerance toward intolerable student misbehavior. Indeed, just the opposite is true. Intolerable behavior must be stopped, and generally, it must be done as quickly as possible. This principle simply means that while the teacher is doing everything in his power to try to teach the child how to behave more constructively, he has to be steadfastly unwilling to give in or give up.

The wise teacher knows that there are numerous ways to teach sound values in behavior, but the best of all possible ways is by modeling them. We teach the value of patience by being patient. We teach the value of rationality by being rational. We teach the value of unselfish love by unselfishly loving. We teach wisdom by behaving wisely.

Because the above ideals are absolutely true, the Christian parent will hold his children's teachers accountable to them whether or not the teachers are aware of these ideals. A conscientious teacher strives to remember that he is being paid to help your child. This is an essential truth for all teachers who wish to be objective, rational, and professional.

It is understandable, though, that even the best teachers may be tempted to forget this fact under the provocative conditions of student misbehavior. Nonetheless, your hard-earned tax dollars should never finance teachers and administrators who inflict serious harm or suffering on your child. You are not paying them to ignore these ideals, nor to forget them, nor to abandon them.

Facts About Teachers and Discipline

All realistic parents know that schools need to be supported. The most common complaint one hears from teachers is that their task of teaching is made very difficult by students who create emotionally embarrassing and harrowing problems of classroom control. The second most common complaint teachers make is that they are seldom adequately supported by administrators and parents. It is an incontestable fact that teaching in public schools in America is a very unstable profession, due primarily to the aforementioned complaints. In two years, twenty percent of beginning teachers quit, disillusioned and bitter. About half of first-year teachers declare openly that they do not plan to be teaching after five years. [1] Much of this is due to lack of talent and maturity. But undoubtedly, some of the failure of beginning teachers is explained by the headaches and heartaches of feeling underappreciated, under-supported, and under-rewarded on the job. Wise and understanding parents will try to do whatever is practical to provide needed support.

Only teachers with first-hand experience know how great the challenges are in a captive audience classroom. Only caring teachers know the difficulty of trying to teach students who aren't interested in learning or who are too lazy to exert the effort required to learn. Only those on "the firing line" know how trying it is to teach in a school where parental and administrative support is weak or non-existent.

Studies have shown that sixty percent of beginning teachers develop negative attitudes toward their students and a distaste for teaching by Christmas of their first teaching year. In fact, many already feel doomed to failure in the profession and have slipped into a basically adversarial kind of relationship with their students, seeing them as enemies.

Teachers need better working conditions, fewer students in their classrooms, higher salaries and much stronger administrative and parental support. They cry out for stronger sympathy and understanding.

Even so, the responsible parent can support only those persons, activities and policies in the schools that are beneficial for the children. Sensible parents want their children to be taught by teachers who are strong but also humane and reasonable models of authority. An integral part of a proper education is a person's ability to distinguish between humane and inhumane, just and unjust kinds of authority in our social institutions. It is learning what kind of authority one has a moral responsibility to comply with versus the kind that one has a right to disobey. The person who cannot distinguish between justifiable and unjustifiable civil disobedience cannot be relied upon to realistically look after his own rights nor to help protect those of his neighbor.

Your Rights and the School's Responsibilities

The courts have ruled repeatedly that it is the duty of the school to enforce the kind of discipline needed to protect a child's right to learn. It is the school's duty to ensure a child's opportunity to learn, free from any form of physical or psychological obstruction. "Students posing a continuing danger to persons or property or an ongoing threat of disrupting the academic process may be immediately removed from school." [2]

However, courts also have ruled that students must be protected from any disciplinary practices that are excessive, vindictive, malicious, or that intend to injure a child. The courts have ruled consistently that teachers and administrators are not free to act capriciously, arbitrarily or unreasonably. The principal guideline which court rulings obligate teachers and officials to uphold in determining disciplinary policies is the "law of reasonableness." It is the only guidance given to school officials when writing rules and regulations. [3]

Since state statutes and court rulings governing discipline vary so much across the country, it is essential for the parent to understand what requirements of discipline have been imposed on the public schools by the Supreme Court. Regardless of the age of your child, he cannot legally be suspended from school except under certain conditions.

(1) Your child is entitled to Procedural Due Process.

Throughout most of America's educational history, schools could expel any student without justifying it to anybody. In 1975, however, the Supreme Court *(Goss v. Lopez)* ruled that

Procedural Due Process obligates the school in two ways. First, it must communicate to the student, both orally and in writing, what charges have been levied against him. Second, it must give the student a chance to defend himself in a hearing.

Beyond these two basic federal requirements, states vary in how they outline the particular liberties that a student may enjoy during his hearing. Some states permit the student to cross-examine witnesses; others do not. Some permit legal counselors to represent the student while others don't. There appears to be no absolute requirement that parents be allowed to be present at all such hearings, although denying a parent this privilege is certainly unwise. What is required of all states is that every student have a chance to "tell his side." The student also must be given adequate time to prepare his case (generally one to five days). States vary in how much time they regard as adequate "appropriate notice" of charges.

(2) The school cannot suspend your child without being able to justify its action.

For your child's suspension to be "reasonable," school officials must be able to show that it does not violate the statutes of the state you live in, nor the statutes of the federal government, nor the rulings of the courts. To be "reasonable," any school disciplinary action against your child cannot violate the Civil Rights Act of 1871 (which guarantees every citizen the chance to defend himself). Nor can it violate the Constitution which broadly defines every citizen's rights.

Sometimes, though, a school has to act against a student's constitutional rights or civil liberties: for example, the right to freedom of speech, the right to assemble, and the right to pursue one's own personal liberty and happiness. When this happens, the school has to be prepared to show to a judge (or in a court trial if it is taken that far), that the denial of the individual's rights was necessary for the sake of the greater good of the school community. In American legal philosophy, no individual can claim rights and liberties that would threaten the overall greater good. To be "reasonable," the school must be able to show that the suspension is necessary to keep order, to maintain an uninterrupted process of learning, and to protect other persons and property in the school.

A student cannot be legally suspended because of bias against his race, religion, political view, economic class or harmless differences in his personality.

"Student rights are based on the Fourteenth Amendment to the Constitution. To deprive any person of life, liberty [in this case, liberty to get an education] or property without due process and an opportunity to be heard is a violation of the Fourteenth Amendment." [4]

Only the courts can legally decide whether your child's rights have been violated. Unless the decision to suspend a student is challenged in court, it stands as legal. If a student does challenge the school, then the burden of proof that he has been illegally treated falls on his shoulders. Since, of course, most students' cases are managed by their parents' lawyers, the burden actually falls on them.

Courts have generally ignored student challenges of school decisions unless the student has first exhausted all possibilities of achieving a remedy through internal due process within the school. If the court decides that the student's rights were negligently disregarded by the school, or, if it decides that the motivation behind the suspension was malicious, then it may award money to him for damages.

All of the above remarks have applied specifically to *suspension*. "Suspension" and "expulsion" in some states are defined in different ways. If a child is put out of school for only a short time (up to ten days), then that is generally termed a "suspension." But if he is put out of school for more than ten days, that is generally termed an "expulsion." Court rulings have implied that there is even more need for rigor in procedural due process for a period extending over ten days (expulsion) because of the gravity of the action. [5]

In recent years there has been much controversy over the

wisdom of corporal punishment as a method of disciplining students for misconduct. Legally, this term is defined as the use of physical force in any form to inflict pain upon a student for behavior that is against school regulations. In two different decisions the Supreme Court has upheld the legality of the practice by leaving it up to each state to decide for itself whether it will be permitted and under what conditions. [6] Today, corporal punishment is outlawed in the states of Hawaii, Massachusetts, New Jersey, New York, Rhode Island, and Vermont. In most other parts of the country, corporal punishment is not prohibited by law but may be prohibited or limited by state or local school board regulations.

As the result of various court rulings, the following guidelines generally apply for judging the legality of physical force:

(1) *It must be used to improve the student's conduct only after other methods have failed.*

(2) *It must not be excessive.* One teacher was successfully sued for breaking a boy's arm. The court ruled that the use of physical force went beyond a "reasonable degree" because it was unnecessary to achieve the desired end and caused needless injury. [7]

(3) *It must do no abiding harm.* The courts have upheld inflicting temporary suffering (e.g., stinging a child's posterior from spanking), but to inflict lasting injury, either physical or psychological, is to invite litigation. A Pennsylvania court ruled in favor of a student who was "struck on the head, knocked against the blackboard and furniture, and subjected to ridicule during class." [8]

(4) *It must comply with state laws.* In a state where corporal punishment is forbidden, physical force is legal only when it can be shown to be "reasonable," to protect oneself, others or property from needless damage.

(5) *It must not make any unreasonable use of instruments.* For example, in one case a paddle three inches wide and twenty inches long was deemed to have been used excessively, creating

84

psychological trauma involving medication, and was not upheld." [9]

(6) *It must contain no malicious motivation.* Teachers who paddle a child meanly and sadistically will not be supported in the courts. The teacher *cannot legally use physical force with anger.* One teacher was successfully sued because in a fit of anger he struck a student on the ear and burst his eardrum. [10]

(7) *It must apply reasonably to the age and sex of the student.* It is generally unreasonable for a male teacher to spank a high school girl, or for a female teacher to spank a high school boy.

These are not universal legal absolutes, but they are well recognized legal precedents. If no harm is demonstrably done by a deviation from this standard, then a court may uphold it under the legal principle of *in loco parentis.* That is, if the court would uphold a parent doing it, then it would uphold a teacher doing it under circumstances that are identical.

Other Punishments: Legal or Illegal?

Another controversial area of discipline is that which involves the use of "sanctions." To employ sanctions is to punish a student by depriving him of a privilege. For example, pupils in elementary school generally enjoy the privilege of going outside to recess as a break from sitting in the classroom. It is generally considered reasonable to deny a pupil this privilege as a tactic for motivating him to improve his behavior. It can be reasonably argued that recess is a behavioral privilege that has to be earned on an ongoing basis.

However, sanctions may involve denying a student credit for something that he has already earned. This practice has resulted in many suits. In most cases, the courts have ruled against the teacher (or administration) on the grounds that it is unreasonable to take from a student that which is legitimately his. For example, students cannot be denied credit for knowledge they already demonstrably possess, or for skills they have acquired, or for privileges they have already earned.

85

A parent would be wise to be aware of these illegal uses of sanctions:

(1) Denying a student the right to graduate as punishment for misbehavior. Of course, this assumes that the student has learned all that he has been required to learn in order to be entitled to graduation according to the school's rules. [11]

(2) Lowering a student's academic grade as punishment for misbehavior. The courts have not been altogether consistent in this ruling. This practice is illegal unless it is provided for by the statutes of the state. To operate legally, a school can do only that which the state statutes specifically authorize or empower it to do. [12]

(3) Denying a student a transcript showing credits for courses he has successfully completed.

(4) Denying a student a deserved promotion.

(5) Denying a student's right to give a valedictory speech because he has a mohawk haircut.

(6) Lowering a student's grade because of unexcused absences. The courts have contradicted themselves in this. The practice was upheld by an Illinois court but was ruled against by a Kentucky court.

(7) Denying a girl the right to graduate, or other privileges, because she has become pregnant. We know of no state which gives statutory authority to discriminate against pregnant girls in school.

(8) Denying married students the right to extracurricular activities (e.g., serving in the student government).

The Supreme Court has not addressed the question of punishment if a child refuses to conform to a dress code or haircut regulation, and the lower courts have given differing answers. The issue would turn upon the reasonableness of the rule, the extent to which it interferes with personal liberty, and the ability of school officials to demonstrate that the rule is necessary for school purposes such as discipline, safety or sanitation.

Also, generally the school cannot discipline a child for

publishing objectionable material in the school newspaper unless the material is legally obscene or likely to cause disruption that cannot be controlled in other ways.

Your Child's Right to Personal Privacy

Another very sensitive area of discipline has been that of "search and seizure." Over the years, many cases have been tried over the question of whether the search of a student has been illegal because it was without "probable cause," and because it was conducted without a search warrant.

Until recently, the law was not clear about the authority of school officials to conduct searches and seizures of property and students in the schools. Courts have wrestled with such questions as whether students have a reasonable expectation of privacy on their persons and in their desks and lockers, and whether school officials are in fact acting as law enforcement officers when they conduct searches.

On January 15, 1985, the Supreme Court issued what may be a landmark ruling on the subject. In the *New Jersey v. T.L.O.* case (so named because juvenile names are usually kept confidential in court records), the Court ruled that a school official need not have a warrant or even "probable cause" to conduct a search. The only requirement is that the search be "reasonable"; that is, that the school official have a good reason to conduct the search and that he not conduct it in an unreasonable manner. A good reason for search would be evidence or information leading the school official to believe the search is likely to uncover something that threatens the proper functioning of the school and the well-being of those in it such as a dangerous weapon, alcohol, narcotics, marijuana, unsanitary foods, hazardous materials, stolen items, or hardcore pornography.

Of course, the reasonableness of the search would also depend upon the manner in which it is conducted. For example, a strip search would almost certainly require probable cause, and in almost all instances would have to be conducted by members of the same sex. "Probable cause" means that the searcher has knowledge, or at least good information to believe, that the search *probably* will result in finding the illegal thing that is suspected.

Also, the search must be "justified at its inception." That is, *before* he conducts the search, the official must have reason to believe his search will turn up something illegal or harmful. He may not search for drugs, find drugs, and then use the drugs he found to establish retroactively the reasonableness of his search. However, drugs found during a search might provide valid reason for further searches of other persons or places.

This ruling strikes a real balance between the students' legitimate need for privacy and the school's right to prevent threats to its educational effectiveness and social soundness.

Christian parents can be grateful for this ruling. While occasionally it may result in an unjust invasion of privacy, in general it should make the public schools a safer place for our children—safer from drugs, violence, and pornography.

In the past, many school officials have been too timorous in pursuing their obligation to protect innocent students. They have been fearful of being bombarded with suits or threats of suits. Most administrators are grateful that the Court has recognized them as insightful professionals who will use their ruling to the greater benefit of students, teachers, and the community. Serious Christian administrators will prayerfully consider all actions involving such searches lest the right be abused.

The latest ruling does not diminish the necessity for vigilance and awareness of abuses, however. On the contrary, since the schools have more liberty than ever to search, it calls for increased student and parent heedfulness. Listed below are some of the more serious possible abuses of school searches:

(1) Multiple searches that have continually turned up nothing, yet the searches continue for their harassment value.

(2) Searches that do not respect the student's privacy, so that personal items such as pictures, letters, and underwear are

passed around or used mockingly in talk about the student.

(3) Searches designed solely to demonstrate the raw power of teachers and administrators to make disliked students feel helpless and worthless, and desirous of leaving school.

(4) Searches which force a student to remove his clothing on the pretext of an ungrounded suspicion of finding something illegal on the person. In one case, a student was stripped naked and searched. The court "deplored the indignity done the student by forcing him to strip" and pointed out the possible psychological damage that can be done to a sensitive young person. [13] Even with probable cause, school officials have been admonished by the courts to be extremely prudent and circumspectful in such searches.

It may seem incredible to some readers that any such searches can go on in the schools at all. But the record shows that they do. For example, "teachers of a fifth grade went too far in conducting a strip search for $3.00 reportedly stolen from another student. The court held that the search went too far in subjecting *all* students to it." [14]

Illegal Punishments

In general, listed below are examples of abusive school punishments against which the courts have ruled:

(1) The Board of School Commissioners of the City of Indianapolis denied students their right to distribute literature, disliked by the school, on the school grounds. Their right was upheld by all the lower courts until finally an appeal reached the Supreme Court. There, the case was dismissed because by the time it reached the Court all plaintiffs had graduated, making the question of their rights in that school no longer relevant. Thus, there was no Supreme Court ruling, but the ruling of the last court to hear the case stood as legal precedent. [15]

(2) A student does not have to pay for school property which is damaged accidentally. Unless the damage is done deliberately, there is no infraction of school rules and the student must not be punished. An early Indiana Supreme Court decision noted

that carelessness is common to children and they cannot be punished for it or required to pay for it.

(3) Students have been punished, or expelled, for wearing armbands to harmlessly symbolize a moral and/or political protest. This is, of course, a most basic issue of human rights. The classic trial of *Tinker v. Des Moines Independent Community School District* was the kind of case which taxes the will of people to fight for precious rights. In reading the Court's summary of its opinion, one finds the statement that "neither students nor teachers shed their constitutional rights to freedom of speech or expression at the schoolhouse gate." [16]

The Court ruled for the students, saying that wearing the armbands constituted no disruption of school; hence, the school had no grounds on which to object or to punish. There is an interesting point of irony in this case. It was the Board's action against the students that caused disruption in the school. It also caused much commotion in the community. The school authorities feared that the armbands would cause disruption, but their ungrounded, subjective fear gave them no right to punish students for an infraction they had never committed. To deserve disciplinary action, a student must actually cause disruption. In effect, the Court chided the school for creating a legal hassle that never should have existed. Many lives were deeply, needlessly harrowed.

Swearing at students, calling them names, belittling, taunting, or provoking them are more simple and common kinds of illegal disciplinary abuses. Also, there are much more serious abuses which, thankfully, are far less common. For instance, isolating a student in a dark closet. One claustrophobic student was terrorized to hysteria. Another student was made to run laps until he fell in utter exhaustion, requiring medical care.

Recently, students in one high school were not permitted to go to the restrooms without wearing a commode seat around their necks. Of course, some students felt that this was "just fun"; but some found it humiliating and degrading. Occasionally one hears of a child who is denied a necessary visit to the restroom with the predictable humiliation in the presence of his peers.

Some students have been made to sit alone under the teacher's desk. Some have had chalk and erasers thrown at them. Some have been screamed at, squeezed to the point of being hurt, and humiliated by mockery, ridicule, and scornful laughter. Literally being made to wear a dunce cap has been out for a long time; but being made to feel like a dunce is an experience too many students still undergo.

School Rules: Basic Guidelines

Among experts in effective classroom management, there is broad agreement that all essential school rules should comply with the following standards:

(1) Students must be informed at the beginning of school what the rules are. The most effective way is to hand them the rules in writing.

(2) A rule should be for the benefit of the students. It should protect their well-being and optimize their chances of learning and having good relationships with their teachers and peers.

(3) Each rule should be stated with unmistakable clarity so that it cannot possibly be misunderstood or leave confusion in anybody's mind.

(4) The rule should have a rationale, a constructive reason for it. It should serve a constructive purpose and show how a real life need can be fulfilled by students' compliance. In other words, there must be a need for the rule. If students do not see the reason for the rule or the purpose that is served by it, then complying with it will seem unreasonable, purposeless and needless—and hence senseless. The purpose of the rule should be primarily to fulfill the students' needs, not merely the school employees' desires.

(5) The rule should be practically enforceable in a way that does not create more problems than it solves.

(6) Rules should never be couched in broad abstract generalizations such as, "Do not be disrespectful toward your

teacher." Rather, they should be couched in the language of particulars, such as, "While the teacher is presenting a lesson, do not talk without raising your hand and asking for permission."

Changing the Discipline Used with Your Child

What can you do when you know that your child has been improperly disciplined?

In a teacher-principal-parent conference, you may attempt to calmly and systematically explore a solution to your child's problem in a friendly, non-threatening way. You may describe to the teacher and principal how the form of discipline that is being used is not achieving its ideal end—improving the relationship between the teacher and your child. You may describe to the teacher the negative manner in which your child is responding to the discipline, why it is not working. You are free to attempt to explain your child's nature to the teacher. After all, you ought to know your child better than the teacher. You should know what kind of discipline works poorly with your child and what kind works best. And even if that is not the case, to have dialogues with teachers and administrators about your child's problems is your right.

If your approach to them seems friendly and open at the outset, it is less likely to stimulate a defensive reaction that diminishes the chance of objectivity on both sides. Virtually all teachers can tell stories about being accosted by parents who know nothing at all of the facts about how their children have misbehaved. Some parents are taken in by their children and lack objectivity and sophistication in learning the facts. Children are not always objective or honest in the stories they tell their parents.

But sadly, there are many teachers who are not aware that the most effective kind of discipline in a classroom is preventive discipline. Preventive discipline consists of numerous techniques which are designed to help keep serious discipline problems from arising. The best discipline occurs before the fact, not after the fact. Hence, the incidence of the most serious kinds of discipline problems—defiance, insolence, threats of violence—are greatly diminished.

The greatest technique of preventive discipline is bonding. Bonding takes place when a teacher acts to bring greater feelings of respect and affection into the relationship between himself and his students. Many teachers are not aware of the need to bond with their students. Or perhaps there are many who instinctively feel the need but do not know how to accomplish it. When a teacher and his students are bonded, everyone experiences a sense of well-being, a basic security, a joy in doing the things that he is doing with others. The teacher and his students come into the classroom because they want to, not because they must. They anticipate class with pleasure rather than with dread. And they walk out of the class with a genuine sense of personal accomplishment, glad that they have been in the classroom together.

Bonding brings a sense of positiveness, of warm humanness, into the teacher's relationship with his students. The more value the teacher sees in a student, the more value the student will see in the teacher. The more respect the teacher shows to the students, the more respect they will feel toward him. The more the teacher shows that he cares about his students, the more they will care about him. And the more respect and care they feel for him, the less disposed they will be to create serious discipline problems in the classroom.

Some of the most effective ways of bonding are:

(1) *Talk personally* with the student to discover his interests and aspirations. Doing this enables the teacher to better understand how he can arouse the student's interest. It helps him to connect what he is teaching with the student's unique character and values.

(2) *Listen* to the student, not just hearing his words, but trying to hear his heart beat, his soul talk. No student respects a teacher who only wants him to keep his mouth shut and his body still. Real listening demonstrates caring. Students learn to

care about a teacher who first cares about them. Telling them you care doesn't do the job. You first have to show them by the way you treat them. Later on, after they've discovered you are real, telling them will mean something.

(3) *Involve the students* in determining the class rules and goals. Students need to know they have a part in defining the terms whereby they and their teacher will relate with one another. Students are less likely to rebel against rules which they have helped make.

(4) *Use* teaching and testing techniques that, insofar as practically possible, enhance the student's chances of success in learning. Only success in learning can sustain a student's motivation to learn.

(5) *Bring good humor* into the class. Humorless teachers are bores. Also, because they have no levity, they take everything too seriously and overreact. Most students like teachers who will "kid" with them. A little jesting and bantering, always keeping it good-willed and humane, helps to personalize an otherwise formal relationship.

(6) *Share* yourself with the students. Great teachers always give greatly of themselves. If the teacher shows nothing of his inner self and confides nothing about himself, then neither will his students confide in him. Some students feel they cannot confide in their peers or parents. They desperately need someone whom they can trust with their personal feelings and problems.

(7) *Expect your class to succeed.* Deep inside, all students *want* a teacher who will draw the best out of them. They will respect and admire a teacher only insofar as he succeeds in doing just that.

(8) *Give personal talks* to students. Students never fondly remember what they learn from textbooks. They fondly remember only things of special value that a teacher offered them which could not be found in any textbook. Those teachers who are most remembered by their students are those who interestingly and penetratingly talked about life.

(9) *Tell stories.* There is no better way to deeply interest or enthrall students. There is no better way to teach values. By telling dramatic and realistic stories, values can be taught by influencing how a student thinks and feels. Storytelling (the best ones being true ones) enables the teacher to instill values without preaching, lecturing or sermonizing. A few great stories, filled with insight and feeling, sometimes can do more for students than a hundred banal sessions on Values Clarification.

(10) *Appeal to the best* in students. This is the only way students will feel stimulated and challenged to give their best to themselves and their teacher.

(11) *Call students by their first names immediately.* No student will feel the teacher cares about him if the teacher doesn't even know his name.

(12) *Speak* to students *in a deferential tone.* This should be done even to preschoolers and kindergartners. No one likes to be talked down to or addressed in a non-caring tone. The most respected and beloved teachers are known for their respectfulness and consideration.

(13) *Level* with students. A classroom should have an atmosphere of realness. But it cannot unless the teacher comes across as real. Students themselves want to learn to be real. They want to be in the presence of a teacher who is a model. All great teachers are honest with their students. They look into students' eyes and touch them with their spirit.

Of what value is this "teacher talk" to parents, especially to parents whose children may be the victims of teachers who don't know how to bond? Very simply, in approaching a teacher it sometimes can be helpful to first try being soft-spoken and friendly. (Remember Proverbs 15:1.) Many parents make the mistake of appearing hostile and threatening. You can be strongly on the side of your child, yet not begin reproachfully or abrasively. Even the best teachers, when they are tired and tried, sometimes respond defensively to parents who are angry and condemnatory. If you are objective, realistic and positive, kindness can be contagious.

You may need more than one conference to effect a significant change in the way a teacher sees and relates with your child. You may want to invite the teacher to lunch or for a Saturday brunch in your home. Even if your own child is having no trouble with his teachers, you may want to influence the philosophy of discipline operating in the school for the benefit of other children. You might consider it practical to photocopy the list of bonding principles, present them to the Parent-Teachers Association, and request that the chairperson give them to the principal for distribution to all of his teachers.

Of course, there can be no guarantee that this will do any good. There are teachers and administrators who regard even the most diplomatic and friendly efforts to help them as offensive interference. But, there are also those who are open, need to be helped, and are not hamstrung by ego deficiencies that prevent them from receiving help. There is always the chance that you can help. If you don't succeed, then at least you will know that you tried. If you want a teacher to bond with your child, then try bonding with the teacher.

Chapter 6

Ethics and Morality: Your Child's Right To a Safe, Wholesome Atmosphere

Archie Hoflicker is a twelve-year-old boy in the sixth grade. Archie is known by his teachers as a "professional bully." Hardly a day passes without his assaulting one or more of his peers, both with words and his fists. Like most bullies, Archie seldom picks a fight with a bigger boy. When he does, it is only after he has carefully determined that he will prevail over his opponent who, though he is bigger, is judged to be weaker and less skilled in physical combat. When a bully provokes a fight with someone bigger than himself, he usually does it for the same reason that he baits smaller boys to fight—to wrest by force the attention and respect that he does not know how to earn any other way.

Of course, there can be many reasons behind the act of bullying. As a matter of fact, however, most fights in school are not the result of provocation from a "professional" type of bully. Rather, fighting most often arises from short term flare-ups of hurt feelings (often unintended), accidents, hapless misunderstandings, and impetuous comments and actions arising out of normal immaturity. Any experienced teacher or parent knows that fighting can originate among friends as well as among loving children within the same family. The best boys and girls, with the best parents, are capable of irritating one another. Children may inadvertently create frustration, tension, and resentment through the utterance of poorly considered remarks

97

that are not motivated by any real desire to embarrass or injure. Among children, as well as among junior and senior high adolescents, impetuosity sometimes is the order of the day.

A certain amount of fighting is normal, both in the streets and in the school. Thus, the realistic Christian parent will expect it, will not be unduly surprised, and will not flail at the teachers and administrators for "allowing" fighting. Human nature being what it is, there is a certain amount of violence that no degree of preventive measures can avoid—even among adults.

If there is more fighting and bullying than can be reasonably expected and tolerated, however, you may want to consider joining the Parent-Teacher Association (PTA). Through its influence, the school board and administrators can be encouraged to take effective action to stop fighting and bullying. If you can get no effective help from the PTA, organize your own group of parents who share your complaints. Work through them to influence the school officials. You should not feel shy about going directly to the school board. Board members are often politicians with an eye toward re-election and thus want to maintain a positive public image.

If they appear unresponsive to your complaints, you may have to expose the truth to the press about the wrongs which are permitted to happen at your child's expense. The release of group reports to the press is always more effective than a single signature letter to the editor. In most states, school administrators do not have tenure. They realize that bad press constitutes bad public relations, and hence, a very real threat to their jobs.

Some administrators feel paralyzed when it comes to stopping widespread violence in their schools. If this appears to be the case in your community, you or your group may do the following things:

(a) Suggest that school officials (if not the board) bring in professional consultants who are experts on minimizing aggressive behavior.

(b) Suggest that all school officials, teachers, and student leaders attend in-service training and planning sessions to develop a plan for combating the problem.

(c) Suggest that school assemblies be held where detailed attention is given to the problem and to an organized plan for solving it. Individual teachers with strong personalities and effective human relations skills can stop it in their own classes, but only a unified effort of the entire staff and student body can effect far-reaching changes.

(d) Suggest the administration bring in assembly speakers who are looked upon by the students as heroes. Students are more prone to listen to people whom they greatly admire or idolize. When a highly respected hero figure tells why he looks down on fighting and bullying, belligerent students are more likely to be positively affected.

(e) Suggest that substantive discussions be held on the motives that govern the behavior of persons given to violence.

Even in the first grade, such discussions can be quite productive. The discussions, of course, must be carefully guided by the teacher. Students must feel assured that they can express their feelings and ideas without opening themselves to embarrassment or abuse.

Sociodramas or spontaneous play-acting can be a very good technique for teaching children the pitfalls of violence. Children in the early years of primary school have a great capacity to learn from vicarious experience. Children could switch roles, at one time acting out the role of the victim, and at another time acting out the role of the bully. To be most effective, the play-acting should be followed by a class discussion of how everyone feels about the threats and injuries of both psychological and physical assault.

However, if your child has been hurt in school, it is your right to take whatever practical action is possible to prevent repeated occurrences. Also, it is your right to help your child learn to defend himself lest he needlessly become the victim of injury.

The child of pacifist parents may be taught to be conciliatory, to diplomatically say and do the right things in order to avoid being naively drawn into a fight. The acknowledgment should be made, however, that even the sweetest and most peaceful children may become the victims of unavoidable brutality unless they have been trained in the art of legitimate self-defense. Quality training in self-defense is one method of enabling a person to successfully defend himself while minimizing the hurt to the brutalizer.

Even without martial arts training, we can take responsible action to minimize threats to our childrens' well-being in our homes, schools, and in the streets.

(1) It is generally a mistake to tolerate violence. The physical and spiritual acceptance of violence encourages it and leads to a more widespread practice of it. In the school, as well as elsewhere in the community, when practitioners of violence meet no resistance they learn that they can get by with it. This reinforces their destructiveness.

Additionally, if a child has been taught that bullying is wrong but continues anyway, he will feel at least unconsciously guilty when he resorts to the unprovoked use of force. The more we encourage a person to violence by ignoring it, the more guilt we create in his psyche. And, consequently, the more prone to destructive behavior he becomes.

The reason for this is simple. Guilt creates feelings of frustration and anxiety. Frustration and anxiety create hostility. And the hostile individual will either act it out inwardly against himself, or he will direct it outwardly against others. The bully makes himself and others his pitiable victims.

(2) During the last two decades the incidence of violence in public schools has reached alarming proportions. According to a study conducted by the federal government in 1978, secondary school students were physically attacked at the rate of 282,000 a month. The risk of physical violence upon junior high school students is even higher. And as alarming as the recorded statistics are, 83 percent of attacks with weapons in

schools are never reported to the police. Forty-two percent of physical attacks result in injury and 83 percent of these injuries are not reported to the police.

Each month 2.4 million secondary students become the victims of theft. Each month 130,000 teachers have their own money or possessions stolen in the secondary schools. In our cities, the most unsafe place teenagers can be is in the schools. Calculating from figures cited in this same report, one concludes that each year in the elementary and secondary schools there are about 1,700,000 burglaries and 6,000 rapes. [1]

About 47,000 high school teachers are physically attacked in a year's time. Approximately 20 percent of those attacked are injured severely enough to require medical treatment. [2] Adding the number of elementary and junior high teachers who are attacked, the figure reaches 110,000 annually.

This government study, conducted by The National Institute of Education, was based on a narrow sampling, but a comparison of the study with others indicates that the government's figures may be quite conservative.

(3) Millions of our children would not go to school at all if they were not compelled to do so by the state. But many of our children are miserable in our public schools. The facts send out a clear warning: 28 percent of students now drop out of public high schools, most of whom will never enroll in any other type of educational institution. In addition, millions of other students do not drop out but their life in the schools is doleful and nonproductive. Drop-outs and unhappy students in school are burdened with a higher rate of alcoholism, juvenile delinquency, mental illness, and addiction to drugs.

Of course, many factors contribute to the unhappiness of children in school. But the daily apprehension that comes from the threat of being physically hurt or socially embarrassed is one factor that is most often cited by children who are privately queried. Some of the authors' own children at times have feared going to school because of the threat of being hurt by an unrestrained bully—not to mention the fear of being humiliated by some teacher's scowl or sarcastic tongue.

Teachers and administrators have a professional and ethical responsibility to safeguard the physical and psychological well-being of your child in school. They also have a legal responsibility to do so. This duty has been repeatedly upheld by the courts whenever it has been challenged. The legal obligation to establish and sustain a school atmosphere in which all children feel safe and secure resides in what is commonly known as the principle of *in loco parentis.* As discussed before, this legal term simply means that while the school administrators and teachers are in charge of your child (in the school, on the school grounds, and en route to and from school), they have the responsibility to do what you as a parent would do to safeguard your child's well-being.

Some teachers and administrators may neglect to honor this duty out of ignorance or oversight without any intentional desire to cause injury to your child. Unquestionably, though, much of the fighting in the schools can be prevented if administrators and teachers take proper steps to prevent it.

The statutes and courts have established clearly that every school board member, administrator and teacher is expected to take reasonable care to avoid acts or omissions which he can foresee would be likely to cause injury. An educator:

... is expected to foresee the possible consequences of an action or a condition and then take measures, where necessary, to remedy them. For example, in the ordinary course of a work day, it may involve removing shattered glass in a corridor, warning students to keep away from workers pruning a large tree, adding supervisors to a bus loading area where fights have recently occurred, or giving special instructions prior to undertaking an experiment in chemistry. [3]

Even so, when inattention to this duty results in significant injury to your child, you have the legal right to file a *tort* suit for any damages which you and your child may have suffered. A tort suit is a suit for "a civil wrong, other than a breach of contract, for which a court will provide a remedy in the form of damages. The wrong grows out of harm to an individual by the unreasonable conduct of others. The remedy is premised on the notion that one should be allowed to recover something, usually money, from the one who harmed him." [4]

When harm is done because of serious—even though unintentional—neglect, the educators may be sued for "compensatory damages." In such a case the victim may recover the money he or his parents have lost, i.e., the cost of all the damage done. However, if the neglect of duty has been "gross" (willful, wanton or intentional), the neglectful person may be sued for "punitive damages." If you win a suit for punitive damages, the court will decide how much money you will be awarded based on the extent of the harm done and the depth of malice in the guilty party.

Laws that make punitive damages possible have not been enacted to encourage the spirit of revenge. Rather, they have been enacted as a realistic recognition of human nature. There are always some who will take immoral advantage of you, even subject you to potentially fatal injury, and will do it without (apparently) the slightest misgivings or compunction.

For example, an automobile manufacturer may know that he is selling cars with built-in defects which can cost a life. He may not wish to pay for the correction of these defects because it would lower his profits. Until costly and effective punitive measures are levied on him for such wrongdoing, he will close his eyes to the tragedy and potential tragedy for which he is responsible. Suits for compensatory damages or punitive damages are allowed, and, in fact, encouraged by the law for the sake of justice and to send a warning to potential wrongdoers.

To Sue or Not to Sue

When a Christian has been wronged in such a manner, suing for punitive damages is not hypocrisy. When Jesus sent out His

103

disciples to win the world, He specifically warned them: "Behold, I send you out as sheep in the midst of wolves; therefore be shrewd as serpents and innocent as doves" (Matthew 10:16). Although given specifically to His disciples, there is an application in this for us today. As important as it is to treat others gently, it is equally as important to be wise and to act when necessary.

If the damage done to your child and/or to you is a small amount of money, you may sue for what is called "nominal damages," i.e., damages "in name." In other words, you may sue simply as a matter of principle, without a desire to collect any meaningful sum of money. We know of one individual who won a suit for nominal damages and was awarded the sum of $1.00. The person then paid $3,000 for the service of his attorneys, but seemed to be satisfied in saying, "I made my point." Clearly the only legitimate purpose in filing such a suit is to right a wrong in principle. Under appropriate conditions, you may wish to file such a suit to help teach a needed moral lesson to someone who otherwise would continue to carelessly hurt others.

However, we do not recommend taking anyone to court without an earnest, concerted effort to solve the problem in other ways. There can be no mistaking the fact that a Christian cannot sue for undeserved and unneeded personal gain, nor for revenge or spite. The thoughtful Christian will try earnestly to avoid a court case regardless of the damages. Even when one is entitled to compensation for harm suffered, he will make every reasonable attempt to settle the matter out of court without venom. No lawsuit can be conducted in the Christian spirit unless the plaintiff wants only to see that (a) a reasonable and just remedy is accomplished, and (b) any dutiful action taken is to help prevent others from becoming needless victims.

The plaintiff who takes Jesus seriously cannot initiate a lawsuit with any motive other than that of trying to render help where it is most needed. He must be free of the spirit of revenge and the pseudo-luxury of resentment. But when a victim truly deserves help, through monetary compensation reasonably due him, he should seek that help.

In determining whether or not to file suit against a school system or its officials, several Scriptures should be considered. Paul says in I Corinthians 6:1-7(NASB):

> Does any one of you, when he has a case against his neighbor, dare to go to law before the unrighteous, and not before the saints? Or do you not know that the saints will judge the world? And if the world is judged by you, are you not competent to constitute the smallest law courts? Do you not know that we shall judge angels? How much more, matters of this life? If then you have law courts dealing with matters of this life, do you appoint them as judges who are of no account in the church? I say this to your shame. Is it so, that there is not among you one wise man who will be able to decide between his brethren, but brother goes to law with brother, and that before unbelievers?

Paul is speaking about lawsuits between Christians, and perhaps, more particularly, about lawsuits between Christians in the same church. By implication, however, the passage contains a secondary application which requires Christians to make an effort to settle their disputes with the outside world. As Paul says in Romans 12:18: "If possible, so far as it depends on you, be at peace with all men." We are to do our part to resolve disputes amicably, but the very phrase "if possible" implies that it is not always possible. At times the best way to peaceably resolve a dispute might be to refer it to a court for consideration.

Jesus explained the Scriptural method of solving a dispute between Christians in Matthew 18:15-17:

> And if your brother sins, go and reprove him in private; if he listens to you, you have won your brother. But if he does not listen to you, take one or two more with you, so that by the mouth of two or three witnesses every fact may be confirmed. And if he refuses to listen to them, tell it to the church; and if he refuses to listen even to the church, let him be to you as a Gentile and a tax-gatherer.

(1) After being hurt, go to the one who has harmed you and

seek to achieve an understanding or settlement through private dialogue.

(2) If he is unwilling to hear you, bring one or two Christians with you who can witness on your behalf.

(3) If he still will not hear you, take the matter before the church.

(4) If he will not listen to the church, the church may discipline him after which you may seek resolution of the dispute with him as you would with an unbeliever.

Like I Corinthians 6, this passage speaks of disputes between professing Christians, and it may presuppose that the two Christians belong to the same church. To what extent this may apply to a dispute with a non-Christian or with a secular institution like a school district is open to question. Obviously the non-Christian or the school district would not submit to the jurisdiction of your church. However, the principle of confronting the wrongdoer personally on a one-to-one basis before taking further action is one which could be applied to almost any dispute. By doing so you give him the opportunity to back down gracefully whereas before a group he might feel compelled to stand firm even if he knows he is wrong. And, it is possible that he is not wrong after all; he may have an explanation for his actions which will satisfy you. This will save you embarrassment, too.

However, none of these passages means you cannot sue a non-Christian or a secular institution. On several occasions Paul asserted his legal rights as a Roman citizen before the civil authorities (Acts 16:35-40; Acts 20:22-29). We have a right to do likewise when the situation requires it. But, most prospective litigants do not realize what a toll a lawsuit takes on all parties involved in terms of financial costs, emotional trauma, time consumed and fractured relationships. Seldom is there a real winner.

Your Child's Rights to Physical and Emotional Security in School

Most school districts have formal policies which address your legal right to inspect your child's school for any physical or social conditions which you suspect are threatening to your child. You are paying for the school, the equipment, the upkeep, and the educators' salaries with your taxpayer's dollars. The school exists for your child. Your child is not there for the educators' sake; rather, they are there for your child's sake. If you have sound reasons to believe that a teacher is harassing your child, you may request permission to sit in the classroom and observe. In accordance with your school's policies, you may also observe in the music room, study hall, lunchroom (where most fights break out), in the restrooms or anywhere else.

You also have the right to request a meeting with any teacher or school board official whose decisions directly affect your child's life. Also, you may request a meeting of school personnel with a group of parents who want to discuss a common matter. In many jurisdictions this is your right as a matter of law; in others it is school policy to honor such requests by providing a time and place for such a meeting.

You may also expect educators to respond to your communications in writing. For example, if you have requested that effective measures be taken to curtail fighting and to put an end to bullying, then you may request to be informed in writing of what measures are being taken toward this end. Usually this request will be honored.

Either as an individual or as a group, you may question, evaluate, and criticize any policies or actions (or lack of them) which you believe are having an unwholesome affect on your child's educational development and personal soundness.

One fact is paramount in the law and in the court rulings: the school has an inviolable obligation to provide environmental conditions that are *conducive to learning*. Thus, if a child is being psychologically hurt in a way that significantly obstructs learning, the school has a responsibility to act effectively to remove the source of that hurt. And this is true whether the hurt is being caused by teachers or by students.

The school has a responsibility to protect your child from theft. Theft results in the loss of property needed and perhaps cherished by the child; it also may result in significant damage to him emotionally. In fact, seldom is a person the economic victim of theft without being the emotional victim of it. Being the victim of serious theft can give a child a profound sense of helplessness. While a school cannot be expected to guarantee against all theft, the school could possibly be held liable in court if the theft were found to have been caused in part by negligent supervision or inadequate preventive measures.

Also, the school has the responsibility to shield your child from any damage that might be done to him by students being allowed to use and disseminate alcohol, marijuana, drugs or deadly weapons in the school. While no school can guarantee that a student will learn, the school is obligated to provide both physical and psychological conditions which ensure him the opportunity. The school has the duty to effectively discipline any student who is obstructing this opportunity, and to supervise and oversee its own employees to ensure that they will not obstruct your child's opportunity to learn.

In recent years several educational malpractice suits have been filed in various parts of the country, alleging that a school is negligent because a child has failed to learn. However, to date none has been ultimately successful. The courts' reasoning seems to be that it is difficult to determine what constitutes bad teaching, and it is equally difficult to determine that bad teaching is the cause of failure to learn. Some children may fail or refuse to learn even under ideal teaching.

The "law of reasonableness" implies that a school employee is not free to abuse your child psychologically or emotionally with ridicule, mockery, taunting, baiting, browbeating, harassment, undue psychological pressure of any injurious form, or with any other form of verbal assault. Likewise, the school is legally obligated to take reasonable action to prevent any students from frustrating or hurting your child in any way that obstructs his opportunity or impairs his ability to learn.

It would be unrealistic to assume that any school can provide a perfect environment in this respect. But it would be equally unrealistic to assume that when your child is hurting you can do nothing about it. While court precedents protecting a student's rights in this regard are scant, the fact is unchallengeable that emotional security is essential to optimal learning. This gives you the right to take action just as readily as if your child were being physically abused.

If you don't like the situation your child has been given, you have a right to request his reassignment to another classroom or school within reasonable limitations. Some schools have "open enrollment," which allows you to send your child to any school in the district. If there is no "reasonable" rationale supporting the school's assignment of your child to a particular teacher or classroom, your request for reassignment would probably be upheld by the courts.

However, a school does have the right to hold your child back a grade against your wishes for inadequate academic performance. If such an action occurs, it may be desirable to request a different teacher for your child.

May I demand that certain information be furnished to me from my child's school records?

Generally, yes. The Family Educational Rights and Privacy Act of 1974 guarantees parents and guardians access to school records. The disclosure of personal information without their consent is also prohibited. The law also allows eligible students—and parents of students who are not eligible—to review their records, reproduce their records, and raise questions relative to the accuracy of information in their records. It also provides these persons with the right to control dissemination of information within the record, unless it can be demonstrated that those who are seeking the information have a "legitimate interest" in the requested information. Other than parents or guardians, it is generally held that only interested professionals may have access to school records.

Can my child be grouped in a low ability group, or any other group, without my consent?

Probably yes, with some limits. If the school district is pursuing legitimate educational objectives as the major reason for its ability grouping, and if such grouping was determined through defensible measures of achievement or ability, the school will be allowed wide latitude in grouping your child. However, if your child is placed in a "slow" group without sufficient opportunity to advance out of the group, such placement might be successfully challenged.

If I want to, can I take my child out of public school and enroll him in a private school or teach him myself at home?

Yes. The 1925 U.S. Supreme Court case of *Pierce v. Society of Sisters* guarantees parents the right to send their children to private schools, subject to regulations which vary from state to state. Home schooling is legal in all states except possibly Texas where it is being litigated. (The issue is whether the term "private school" includes a home school, again subject to varying degrees of state regulation.) Some states like North Dakota and Michigan require that all children be taught by certified teachers, which effectively eliminates home schooling as a legal option for all but a few; others like Oklahoma and Illinois allow home schooling so long as children are, in fact, being taught and the home schooling is not simply a subterfuge for truancy. The constitutionality of laws restricting home schooling has not yet been settled, but the trend among legislatures is toward greater recognition of the right to educate children at home. In some states or school districts it may even be possible to teach your children at home and have them participate in certain courses or activities at the public schools. It is important to obtain competent legal advice as to the requirements of your state and district.

Chapter 7

Extracurricular Activities: Playing To Win... Or Playing the Players?

Case Study #1: In Longmont, Colorado, a father threatened the school district with a lawsuit because his son did not earn a football letter. The father claimed that his sixteen-year-old son had been "psychologically and emotionally fractured" by the coaching staff. "The issue," said the father, "is not the letter, but that my son was hurt." The young man was one of four high school football players who did not receive a football letter because they had not played a minimum of 20 quarters during a ten-game season. Can schools give awards to some children and not others for achievement in activities which are extracurricular; that is, activities which are available to enrich the education of children?

Case Study #2: A local high school established a policy, in conjunction with the athletic association of high schools to which it belonged, of charging admission to attend school athletic events. A mother and father who were suffering financial hardships because of the father's loss of his job were forced to stand in a hallway adjacent to the auditorium to watch their seventh-grade daughter participate in an inter-school volleyball game. The reason? They did not say so, but they could not afford the price of admission to the volleyball game. Can schools legitimately charge parents a fee for admission to extracurricular events held on public property under school supervision when the parents' interest and attendance is clearly a desirable help to their children's education?

Case Study #3: The parents of a young girl who had frequently tried out for a part in school dramatic activities threatened to bring suit against the school district. The problem? In tryout after tryout, their child, who admittedly was not a future academy award contender, failed to secure a part in school dramatic presentations. Instead, the child was given mundane and menial tasks in an unsuccessful attempt to mollify her. These included passing out programs for the school play, collecting monies, and cleaning up after the dramatic presentations were over. Does a child have a legitimate right to be included in an extracurricular activity if the child does not meet the teacher's performance standard for inclusion?

Unfortunately, the situations described above and the questions they imply have not been addressed by the courts; therefore no definitive answers can be provided. The whole area of extracurricular activities and your child's rights to participate will remain a gray area until you as a parent begin to express your legitimate interest in your child's total education, including his or her full participation in extracurricular activities.

We're Number One! . . . In What?

"Winning isn't everything, it's the only thing," said Vince Lombardi.

"Nice guys finish last," Leo "The Lip" Durocher claimed.

Unfortunately, these two often and flippantly quoted remarks accurately embody the current philosophy on interschool extracurricular activities in the United States. This is not a new philosophy; it has been the prevailing philosophy for the past several decades. It is a philosophy which is pervasive, encroaching even into other areas of society. One can observe many examples of "We're number one!" including the raised index fingers of fanatical spectators at an athletic event or the uncontrolled exuberation of players at the professional or amateur level who have succeeded in defeating their opponent. Number One. But Number One in what? In popularity? In quality? In adherence to high principles? This key question has not yet been answered in the public schools nor in society as a whole. It can perhaps most clearly be stated with this question: *Do you play your players to win, or do you play to "win" your players?*

In other words, do nice guys, indeed, finish last, as was claimed by Leo Durocher; or do they, in the words of another, greater public figure, finish first? "The last shall be first, and the first last," said Jesus Christ. "The meek shall inherit the earth," He added. "Whoever is greatest," He said, "shall be the servant of all."

Does the We're Number One! philosophy, which too often sacrifices concern for the immature and developing emotions and feelings of children in order to win, allow room for the philosophy of Jesus Christ? This is a question all Christian parents need to address, particularly those who are clients of the public schools. Let's take a look at the ramifications of this question.

The "Stage Parent"

Almost every parent can sympathize with this scene. A child faithfully goes to practice after practice after practice. The child strives diligently for excellence in a sport, sacrificing time with friends, time with family, and time which might have been spent on other equally desirable but less peer-oriented recreational pursuits. Finally, the big day comes. Parents, maybe even grandma and grandpa and other relatives, go to the first game and they suffer in silent agony as the coach selectively plays only a choice few of his players for the sole purpose of winning the game. On the bench, attempting to look cheerful and exuberant, hoping against hope that the coach will notice them, sit several players whose hard work and sacrifices are not rewarded with participation in the game—unless, of course, the game is so clearly won or so clearly lost that their participation is obviously irrelevant.

The message to the student: "You can try and try, but in the final analysis what you have to offer to this team is irrelevancy. Your participation is not relevant. You as a player are irrelevant." What does the parent do? The parent does not want to be a "stage parent"—the kind who is involved in harassing and berating the Little League coach for not putting his child into the game. Yet, *if your child's best interests are at stake, at what point should you do precisely that?* You know your child has worked hard. You know that he wants above everything else to be a valued participant. You know how your child is suffering emotionally by not really being included, or worse yet, by being ignored or even disparaged by a coach whose sole intent is winning. You know that the other players in the peer group, whose approval is so important to a child, are looking with less-than-admiring eyes at the sub sitting on the bench or standing in the wings. You know that this exclusion may leave deep scars. And you know that as the top performers get the opportunities to play, they will continue to get better.

And yet, the "winning is the only thing" mentality has been accepted as the norm. Mature adults who should know better have sat silently on the sidelines enduring vicariously the agony of exclusion felt by their children. What can be done about it? Does this condition have to persist or can changes be made?

The Purpose of Extracurricular Activities

No educator would deny that the major purpose of extracurricular activities is to enhance the child's total educational experience. They are available in order to develop the child in activities of secondary importance which are not normally available in the regularly scheduled curriculum. For this reason, participation in extracurricular activities has been held to be a privilege, based upon whether or not the child has met minimal academic standards regarded as absolutely indispensible. But if those certain minimal academic requirements in the indispensible curriculum have been met, and if children are healthy, there seems to be no reason why they should be excluded from full participation in extracurricular activities. The only other reason for excluding children from equal participation would have to be that a winning or a performance oriented mentality is prevalent.

Unless it can be shown that these goals are consistent with the maximal development of each personality, it can be logically argued that an *extracurricular philosophy that discriminates against the less talented for the sake of performing or winning is inconsistent with defensible and desirable goals of public education in the United States.* The courts seem to implicitly recognize this fact by discouraging the transfer and recruitment of students specifically for sports advantages.

If, then, it can be defensibly argued that the "winning is everything" mentality is not consistent with the goals of public education in the United States, it must logically follow that the only other reason for extracurricular activities is to provide each student with *extra* curricular opportunities—growth opportunities which will enhance his development as a productive member of society.

Further, it must also logically follow that to achieve this end, full and equal participation should be granted to each student who desires participation in an extracurricular activity. The only remotely tenable grounds for exclusion would be disciplinary, academic or health reasons, or that the child's unsatisfactory performance level would ultimately detract from the educational experience for all other participants. For example, a child who could not play the violin but insisted upon being included in the school orchestra would obviously detract from the opportunity of all participants in the orchestra to derive maximum educational benefit from a harmonious orchestra performance.

On the other hand, it is not as easily argued that winning is essential to deriving maximal benefits from participation in sports. Therefore, there seems to be no readily apparent reason why an elite group of students should constitute a "first string" while another group of students only "warm the bench" because of a coach's desire to win at all costs.

Sadly, this mentality has led to elitism of the most insidious kind. It is an elitism not only of individuals endowed with athletic ability but also of certain extracurricular activities which leads to the ultimate detriment of other extracurricular activities. Sports are highly funded and athletic ability highly recognized while equally important extracurricular activities are underfunded. Boys' sports are very generously funded which has resulted in many cases in underfunding girls' sports.

The win-at-all-costs mentality leads to losses all the way around! Loss of proper perspectives on why school sports exist. Loss in opportunities for the overall development of character, perseverance, and athletic skills for those students who most need improvement. Loss of opportunity for coaches and instructors to meet individual needs because of their need to satisfy the accepted expectations of victory. This attitude has lodged itself into the public mind. Even Christian parents do not challenge potentially destructive statements of public school philosophy, such as the "Activities Program" brochure of the Denver (Colorado) Public Schools:

THE ATHLETIC PROGRAM

A great tradition for athletes is not built overnight. It takes the hard work of many people over many years. Through the years, Denver teams have won many league, tournament, and state championships. Many records have been set by individuals gaining distinction in district and state competition.

Our tradition has been to participate in such a way that honor comes to our athletes, our schools, and our community, and is worthy of the best efforts of all concerned.

As a member of an interscholastic team, you inherit

responsibilities. Your role in contribution to such athletic tradition will undoubtedly be a source of satisfaction not only to your school but to you personally.

Incongruously and contradictorily, the brochure includes this statement of purpose on its front page:

The purpose of this brochure is to encourage all pupils who are entering senior high schools to participate in "STUDENT ACTIVITIES . . . THE OTHER HALF OF EDUCATION"

Attitudes of helpfulness and cooperation are lost when students are placed in competition for a few select positions of prominence. Emphasis on academic achievement suffers with a primary focus on transitory athletic performance.

Are school athletic programs wrong then? Emphatically, no! One of the authors was for a long time a successful coach. Only the destructive results of that mentality are wrong. He asserts without equivocation that, were he to return to the coaching ranks, he would sacrifice winning seasons, trophies, championships and accolades to the higher goal of developing and allowing each player the satisfaction of healthy competition without the pressure to win.

However, a student can be denied the right to play on an athletic team because of a disciplinary incident, if the incident was sufficiently serious and related to athletics. Nevertheless, a federal district court in Arkansas recently ruled that a high school senior's privilege of participating in interscholastic athletics is a property right protected by the Fourteenth Amendment. Since that amendment provides that no state may deprive any person of life, liberty or property without due process of law, the school district must give the student "due process" before denying him the right to play football. Due process would probably include at least an informal hearing, an explanation of why he was removed from the team, and an opportunity to contest the allegations or present reasons why he should be retained.

Refocusing: What You as a Parent Can Do

So firmly entrenched is the mentality of winning that it will take the concerted effort of many parents and public educators to dislodge it. It will take more than one or two parents with the courage to question their children's coaches or to assert their opinions to the school principal. It will take a refocusing of vision, meetings, letters, input from significant people in the community, sound documentation, and an outright demand on the part of the parents for full participation for *all* students who want to participate. Suggestions for accomplishing this are found in the reference, "How to Start an Excellence in Education Committee in Your District."

Equality of educational opportunity would not exist if students who were less proficient than their peers in the regular curriculum were not allowed full participatory opportunity. Just as equal opportunity for participation in learning is provided, so, too, must the opportunity for team work be given in an environment free from an elitist emphasis on winning simply for the sake of winning.

Other Questionable Extracurricular Emphases

With the influence of traditionalists in the public schools has come an increasing clamor for homework. Homework has been cited by various excellence in education committees as a panacea for virtually all of the ills extant in American public schools today. Homework has been demanded by business leaders. "More homework" has been the clarion call of Christian-oriented groups who see it as evidence of more stringent standards in public schools. The presumed benefits of additional homework have been accepted without question by even the most perceptive of parents, and yet the detrimental effects of increased, unnecessary homework far outweigh any potential advantages, *especially for children of Christian parents.* The following situations may illustrate the point.

119

Situation: Christian parents may wish to take their child to a church-sponsored activity or to send their child for spiritual training such as confirmation, youth group, or evening Bible study. A conflict arises. The child who has been assigned homework, in response to parental demands for more homework, is unable to attend the church-related activity or to receive the benefits of spiritual training because of the academic penalties if the homework is not completed.

Situation: A particularly outstanding theatrical production or other edifying educational or spiritual program is presented on television. The family gathers to watch and to discuss the concepts presented. The child cannot participate. His teachers have been pressured to give him homework, and he must pursue a mundane and not even remotely value-comparable assignment in order to satisfy school requirements. The school has, by invitation, entered into and interfered with family communication.

Situation: Parents wish to visit grandparents and to take the children along, a time to strengthen family relationships and to honor the elderly. It's a primary opportunity to glean benefits from the wisdom of grandparents. Problem: the child cannot go along. Reason? Homework. By invitation, the school has disrupted highly desirable family activity.

Situation: The local community college offers a course in water color painting, aerobics, basic masonry, ceramics, or other nonacademic pursuits. Mother and father would like to attend the class. It presents an opportunity for the child to attend the class with the parents and to learn together. The instructor is well qualified. It is a worthwhile educational opportunity. The child cannot participate. The reason? Homework. Demanded by the parents. By invitation, the school has interfered with the parents' opportunity to select educational experiences.

Situation: A part-time job is available. A job for which financial compensation is offered, and one in which rudimentary skills can be learned which are transferable to other jobs. The child cannot participate. Because of homework, a wonderful growth experience has been lost.

Situation after situation can be described, but the point is clear. Homework can often interfere with activities which are far more beneficial to the child than extended schoolwork. Homework has been insisted upon by parents in many cases to teach children responsibility or to keep them off the streets. Yet the teaching of responsibility, while it can be a legitimate function of the schools, is primarily a function of the home. Keeping children productively engaged is also the responsibility of the home. It is not the responsibility of the school to control the hordes of kids wandering around shopping malls or hanging around video arcades. If parents uncritically demand more and more homework, the end result will be the extension of the tentacles of the public school into every area of parental responsibility. The home will be invaded and spiritual development will be pushed aside.

Numerous other facts challenge the desirability of increased homework. The demands upon a child's time are often incredible. He may need to be at the school bus stop by 7:00 a.m. He may ride a school bus for an hour. His whole day may be occupied with classes and with extracurricular activities. He may not arrive home until 6:00 p.m., at which time he may have music lessons, assignments from church, or a part-time job. He should also have home chores to do.

If parents demand more homework and pile other responsibilities upon a child who is already overloaded and who does not have the opportunity for quiet moments of reflection, personal devotion or meditation, or a quiet, peaceful dialogue with mother and father, the parents indeed "know not what they do."

Another factor to consider is that not all children have a quiet area at home in which to study, or parents to help them. On the contrary, some parental attempts to help may degenerate into tension-filled parent/child conflict. Where there is no place to work, children may end up failing because they are circumstantially, rather than academically, unable to keep up. Before demanding more homework, concerned parents should know:

a) *What kind* of homework you want;
b) *How much* homework you want;
c) *The reasons why* you want homework.

Not all homework is valuable. Indeed, homework may be detrimental to the very values, attitudes and behaviors you, as a Christian parent, want to develop in your children.

The most defensible homework for those whose primary concern is the development of spirituality and personal responsibility is precisely that, *home* work: helping one's parents meet the responsibilities and challenges of day-to-day living in contemporary society; addressing the needs of grandparents and relatives; helping neighbors; working at part-time jobs; and doing chores.

As a Christian, you have the right to influence the education of your child by demanding only quality school assignments so that the full influence of the church can be felt by your child and your family. Influence the education of your child by reserving to yourself the prerogative of selecting some of your child's educational activities from community agencies, church groups, community colleges, community recreational organizations and private agencies. Influence your child's education by carefully considering the many opportunities which exist beyond the confines of the school classroom and beyond the influence of a few educators who may not share your perspective of what constitutes valuable knowledge. Influence your schools by demanding very clearly outlined policies on extracurricular activities, including clear-cut policies on the nature, the extent, and the scope of homework assignments.

A Starting Place: Know Your Rights

In order to influence changes in policies governing extracurricular activities, carefully examine the policies currently in existence. For example, most school districts have the state association's statement of policies, rules and regulations concerning the participation eligibility of students in extracurricular activities. In Colorado, for example, the rules, regulations, and related information concerning extracurricular activities, including music, speech, and athletic activities are outlined in a 108 page handbook. Since member schools voluntarily subscribe to and are bound by association regulations, and since it is likely that the courts would uphold an association's right to impose rules and regulations, the state handbook should be studied thoroughly.

In addition to the handbook of the state activities association, a school district will probably have materials available specifying student rights and responsibilities in extracurricular activities. The Denver, Colorado, public schools, for example, provide the prospective extracurricular participant with:

- Rules for Students and Parents, Colorado High School Activities Association (brochure)
- "Handbook for Athletes," a 24 page booklet
- "A Guide for the Approval of Contests and Other Activities," a 39 page booklet
- "Handbook for Pep Club Sponsors," a 22 page booklet
- "Activities" Program brochure for students

These policies are available in any district for the asking. Because of the schools' position *in loco parentis*, the courts have traditionally upheld the schools' right to establish policies governing student rights and responsibilities unless they are clearly unreasonable, arbitrary or violate constitutionally protected rights or state legislated statutes.

For example, in Fort Wayne, Indiana, the Board of Education developed a written set of standards which allows for the suspension of students from after-school activities and also from watching those activities for infractions that occur anywhere or anytime, regardless of whether the violations occur on school property or during a school-sponsored function.

It is best that parents who wish to influence the extracurricular policies of their schools become involved at the policy formulation level rather than challenge policies which are in existence. As a parent, your input on policy formulation is important because the philosophy of a school district concerning extracurricular activities can directly affect both the opportunity and the frequency with which your child will participate. Two examples illustrate this fact:

In Windsor, Colorado, a small community with one high school and one middle school, a lengthy debate ensued over the local policy on athletics when two handbooks—one for students and one for coaches—were submitted to the school board for approval. The debate concerned a set of guidelines for coaches in "cutting" students from athletic teams.

The guidelines, one board member asserted, violated the district's philosophy "to promote the physical, mental, social and moral well-being of participants." A policy which allowed coaches to cut students within two weeks of the official starting date of the sport, and required the coach to deliver in writing to students the criteria for being on the team, was inconsistent with that philosophy, the board member argued.

"We're not that big a district that we need to cut anyone," he said, eliciting agreement from two other board members who nevertheless reluctantly supported the decision of coaches who had helped the administration write the handbook.

"Which is the hottest?" one principal exclaimed. "Cutting students from the program or getting heat from parents of kids not playing?" The superintendent defended the policy on the basis that students are cut from choir and band as well.

Clearly, parent input which challenged or supported a "play only the best players in order to win" philosophy was needed. What is interesting to consider is that both practices—cutting students from an activity *or* making them sit the bench—are open to challenge on the basis of the Windsor district's own stated philosophy on athletics.

A second example of a district's philosophy is evident in a brief statement included in an eight page bulletin entitled, "Extracurricular Eligibility Information Bulletin" of a district in suburban St. Paul and Minneapolis, Minnesota.

> The senior high school athletic program in the Anoka-Hennepin District is primarily for senior high school students. It provides opportunities for athletically gifted students to develop skills and competitive experiences at levels suited to their abilities.
>
> The junior high school athletic program is broad-based and experiential in nature. It provides opportunities for students to gain fundamental and higher level skills of play in addition to the development of social skills relating to concepts of team play, sportsmanship and competition. The program is intended to serve the majority of junior high age students.
>
> However, the Anoka-Hennepin School Board recognizes that there are a few junior high age students whose athletic abilities and emotional development are such that participation at the senior high level is in the best interest of the student. When it is determined to be in the best interest of the student, a ninth grade student may participate in senior high level athletic activities subject to guidelines and procedures governing this matter.

The statement obviously excludes some senior high school athletes. The philosophy embodied in the statement implies that winning is of primary importance; otherwise, those not considered "gifted" could be readily included. At the junior high school level, however, it can be inferred that the philosophy is one which allows for equal opportunity to both practice and play in competitive events. The implication is that all students may participate. Again, the significance of parental participation in formulating policy and in developing philosophies relative to extracurricular activity is an absolute necessity.

Other exclusionary criteria may also apply, such as the newsmaking "no-pass, no-play" policy which requires minimum academic standards, and which was approved by the Texas legislature. It drew thirty court challenges in the spring of 1985, but has been generally upheld. Although thousands of participants were excluded from sports, band and other extracurricular activities; and although thousands of calls jammed the switchboards of the Texas Education Agency, in July 1985 the Supreme Court of Texas upheld the "no-pass, no-play" policy. And in February 1986, the policy was upheld by the U.S. Supreme Court. Criteria established by school authorities will likely continue to be upheld by the courts in the absence of unreasonable and arbitrary conduct on the part of the policy-making board.

Chapter 8

Influence: How To Be Heard In Your Schools

The "Marshmallow Impact": How to Avoid It
Case Study #1: The mother's concern was obviously genuine. Her quavering voice, clenched fingers, and strident tone attested to the fact that her problem was serious. "I just don't know what the problem could be," she blurted. "Last year Shelly was fine. This year, she wakes up with a headache every morning, and she throws up if she has any breakfast at all."

The teacher shifted uncomfortably behind her desk, as though seeking a more secure haven from the jumbled outpouring of the frustrated parent.

"Last year she talked about school all the time," the mother declared, "but this year . . . . " The litany of anxiety continued. The teacher sat, sphinx-like, silently enduring the heated declarations of implicit accusation which, like some searing wind-driven desert sand, eroded the very foundation of her self-confidence. Twenty minutes later, the next set of parents entered an obviously tension-laden conference room. But despite the mother's emotional declaration, nothing had been accomplished and nothing would change.

Case Study #2: "I think more phonics is what we need," the serious-looking man in the corduroy suit tentatively asserted. Encountering no opposition from the school officials, and emboldened by the approval signified by heads in the audience bobbing up and down like wave-rocked channel markers, he increased the volume and the content of his allegation. "There's too much time wasted on unimportant topics, and not enough time spent on the basics!" Glancing from left to right in what would pass in the military as a rapid reconnoitering of forces, he pressed the attack. Other voices emerged from the audience, to echo the allegations of the corduroy-clad catalyst.

Two hours later, the meeting ended. The school district meeting room had served as an emotional litter box for the whole assemblage. But nothing had changed. And nothing would change.

Case Study #3: "I just can't thank you enough for what you've done for Jamie," the mother bubbled. "After the divorce, when his dad left, he was withdrawn, lethargic, and unmotivated. It was that way for a year-and-a-half, and then you came along. What a godsend you were! I just want you to know that I think you are a fantastic teacher, and that you've been not only an instructor, but a real role model as well."

The teacher mumbled a genuine thank you. He was pleased, but embarrassed, by the profusion of compliments. The mother, too, was pleased. She had wanted to tell the teacher how terrific she thought he was, but she had always felt too shy to do it. Now that she had mustered enough courage to express herself, she felt good.

The experience was a highly positive one for both participants. But nothing had really changed. And nothing was likely to change.

Why the Impact of a Marshmallow?

The three situations above illustrate what all too frequently happens when parents assert their rights in the public schools: Nothing. But the reason nothing happens is not the fault of the schools. It is the fault of the parents. Let's look at why the parents' overtures failed, and what we, as parents, can do to really make things happen in our schools. Let's first identify the main barriers to effective communication.

Major Barrier Number One: Seeking Catharsis, Not Change

One serious impediment to parent-to-teacher communication is this: "Asking" a non-question. Let's examine this problem in detail.

In a leading teacher education institution in the west—one with solid accreditation and with equally solid professors—one of the most appreciated topics in a course otherwise devoted to how to teach reading is the subject of how to survive a hostile audience and have a productive parent-teacher conference. Included in the professor's "Ten Commandments of Working with Parents" is this advice: "Thou shalt not answer non-questions."

The main point of the advice is that, when someone makes an accusation, whether it is direct or implied, responding to the accusation is folly. Why? Because the teacher—the accused—can only guess at what the parents'—the accusers'—complaint might be. Likewise, he can only make a guess as to the evidence supporting the complaint. It should be pointed out that the situations described in Case Study #1 and in Case Study #2 above are commonly encountered examples of accusatory non-questions teachers have faced for decades.

A parent's complaint that his child gets sick before school is an old story. Rachel or Robert Regurgitate are the classic caricatures of Everyman's child who, suddenly and inexplicably, is afflicted with an actual physical illness connected with going to school. Rarely considered is the fact that perhaps the child's parents are having domestic problems, or that there are other conflicts the child is facing. Even though the problem could be something not even remotely connected to the classroom, the parents' not-so-subtle message to the teacher is clear: "Something *you* are doing (or not doing) is making my child sick."

It may well be that the parent is right. But such an accusation only identifies a culprit. The accusation is so general that it cannot possibly be answered. Furthermore, it embodies one of the most significant insults that can be hurled at a professional—that, despite a teacher's best efforts, he or she is an abuser of a child's spirit. It is a stinging slap in the teacher's face, an assault on his abilities, on his professionalism, indeed, on his very character. It is impossible in such a situation for the teacher to be open to communication. He will be defensive. If there really *is* a problem with the child, the teacher will not be able to consider it. His understandable and natural defensiveness and the need for professional safety will assume priority in his mind.

The same types of non-questions are evident in Case Study #2, concerning the open meeting in the school administration public auditorium. The man in the corduroy suit did not say anything that required a specific response from the school officials. He accused, and, again, defense mechanisms took over on the part of the accused. Offering an answer to a non-question—to an unsubstantiated accusation—would be foolish on the school officials' part. And in the meeting described, nothing will happen because:

1. *No specific desires* have been expressed;
2. *No specific requests* have been made;
3. *No specific evidence* has been offered.

Such meetings are useful only for venting hostility. When this happens, nothing is accomplished in the way of changing the curriculum.

But all parent-teacher communication isn't negative. In Case Study #3, the situation in which the mother profusely complimented the teacher is every teacher's dream. But it, too, didn't really change anything for the better, at least not to the extent that it could have. A compliment offered to a teacher is like offering him butter for his bread—without a butter knife. To be fully savored, it must be spread around.

The emphasis here is this: If you want to vent bottled up

emotions, buy season tickets for a contact sport. But if you want to make a difference in the schools, work with teachers and administrators for the best interests of your children and our nation. Guidelines can be drawn from both common sense experience and from the uncommon insight of the Scriptures.

Major Barrier Number Two: Forgetting That Teachers Are People, Too.

"_____ are people, too." Fill in the blank with any group you wish, but the truth in the cliche is obvious. Regardless of our calling, we all must manage common anxieties, fears, hopes and desires. Jesus emphasized this most basic truth in Matthew 7:12. And, like most people, the teacher also:

a. Wants to do a good job;
b. Wants his pupils and their parents to like and respect him;
c. Wants to be publicly recognized as capable and professional;
d. Does not want to be the victim of direct or implied accusations;
e. Does not want to be embarrassed in front of other teachers, the principal, parents or pupils;
f. Has concerns about his job security, his paycheck, and his family's needs.

It logically follows, then, that the teacher will seek to ensure his safety if the concerns of parents can be interpreted as a threat to any of his cherished desires. Also, all too often, a teacher must defend himself against unjust actions of school administrators, who also have *their* professional safety to look after. For example, one teacher was told to expect no administrative support in the event of a lawsuit over discipline, and to ignore behavior problems if at all possible.

The solution for parents and teachers is to approach every situation in love.

Effective communication is still possible if the above facts are considered along with these:

a. Teachers are expected to keep track of individual differences in emotional, social, academic and physical maturity for each pupil in classes which often number more than 30 pupils;

b. Under Public Law 94-142 which guarantees every child, regardless of the severity of his disability, an education in an environment which is "least restrictive" to him, and which guarantees parental participation in determining what constitutes such an environment, teachers may be forced to include in their classrooms children who are extremely handicapped mentally, physically or emotionally, and who require constant attention;

c. Teachers may be so restricted by local regulations or by government statutes in administering discipline that, in essence, the schools have run out of ways to discipline students which will not render teachers or administrators vulnerable to successful lawsuits.

Successful positive communication begins with sensitivity toward the concerns, needs, and souls of our brothers and sisters in public education, and the first step toward developing such sensitivity is to divest ourselves of the notion that we are in an adversarial relationship.

Major Barrier Number Three: Failing to Commend With Impact

Dear Mrs. Melchior.

Thank you so much for the extra help you've given to Cathy. She is so positive and enthusiastic about school that we can't believe it.

Walnut Park Elementary School is lucky to have people like you!

Yours truly,

Mrs. Jane Doehrmann

A good step toward making a positive impact with praise has been taken. The parent *put it in writing*. It is as appreciated as the positive comments cited in Case Study #3 at the beginning of this chapter. However, although it is appreciated, it will not have the impact it could have with just *one* minor change. And with *two* minor changes, it could have a tremendous impact.

For greatest impact, a copy of the letter should be sent to the principal with the fact that a copy was sent indicated under the signature, as in the example below:

Yours truly,

Mrs. Jane Doehrmann
cc: Mr. Mark Guhl
    Principal

The principal has now been apprised of your satisfaction. The teacher knows that the principal knows. And the principal knows that she knows he knows. It does sound confusing, but the end result is that the teacher is encouraged to continue the things you appreciate, not only because you like them but because she is aware that the principal has, in effect, been apprised of your expectation. It is positive reinforcement of successful teaching.

As much as a letter of praise sent to the teacher is better than spoken words of praise merely said to the teacher, a letter of praise sent to the principal with a copy to the teacher is even better.

Mr. Mark Guhl, Principal
Walnut Park Elementary School
Sheridan, Wyoming

Dear Mr. Guhl:

I would like to let you know about the wonderful influence Mrs.

Charah Melchior has had on my daughter, Cathy. We have been so pleased . . .

Yours truly,

Mrs. Jane Doehrmann
cc: Mrs. Charah Melchior, Teacher

The letter to the principal, with a copy to the teacher, is more effective because the principal almost *has* to commend the teacher. It would be very difficult for him to fail to say something positive to the teacher because the principal knows that the teacher, who received a copy of the letter, is *expecting* the principal to comment. The letter will also be placed into the teacher's personnel file.

To commend with impact, then:

1. Commend publicly whenever possible;
2. Commend in writing;
3. Commend the person to his or her superior. Hence, the teacher should be commended to the principal, the principal should be commended to the superintendent, and the superintendent to the Board of Education.
4. Send a copy, and note the fact that a copy has been sent, to everyone concerned in the excellence you wish to perpetuate and to all who are in a position to reinforce the actions you are commending. A letter to the principal, therefore, should also show that a copy was also sent to the superintendent.

Major Barrier Number Four: Failing to Criticize With Impact

The letter below is typical of letters of complaint received by principals:

Mr. Al Fischer, Principal
Bellweather High School
Watershed, Wisconsin

Dear Mr. Fischer:

I would like to express my feelings about Mr. Lehrer's attitude toward Mindy. Mindy felt humiliated when she was publicly asked by Mr. Lehrer why she could not serve in the school food booth during the weekend Oktoberfest celebration.
I, for one, do not feel that my daughter's weekend commitments are a matter for public discussion.

Sincerely,

Mrs. Erin Schmidt

Any wise principal would probably respond in one of two ways.

Dear Mrs. Schmidt:

Thank you for your letter expressing your concerns. We find it helpful when parents communicate with the school.

Sincerely,

Al Fischer,
Principal

or

Dear Mrs. Schmidt:

Thank you for your letter expressing your concerns. I would encourage you to follow the Policy on Expressing Concerns outlined in

*the student handbook, p. 12, beginning with contacting Mr. Lehrer
personally to share these concerns with him. I have found him to be
most receptive to communication from parents.*

Sincerely,

Al Fischer,
Principal

Let's analyze how the communication could be improved so
that some actual change takes place, or at least the seeds of
change are planted and have a chance to come to fruition:

First, if a Christian parent has a complaint, the Scripture
provides very clear and precise steps for the resolution of
interpersonal problems.

Step One: Register your concern privately.
And if your brother sins, go and reprove him in private; if
he listens to you, you have won your brother (Matthew
18:15, NASB).

Let the teacher know that you are intentionally keeping your
concern private. Remember that your goal, if you are a Christian,
is to gain a brother as well as to resolve a problem. Be assertive
but non-threatening. Know what you want to accomplish. Be
able to suggest to the teacher the specific course of action you
desire. Chances are, the problem will be solved. If not, take step
two below.

Step Two: Take along a parent who shares your concern as an
observer, or as a "clarifier"; not as an accuser.
But if he does not listen to you, take one or two more
with you, so that by the mouth of two or three witnesses
every fact may be confirmed (Matthew 18:16, NASB).

If, after hearing your concerns validated by the others who
accompanied you, the teacher persists in the behavior which

you perceive to be negative, *and for which you have specific evidence that it is negative*, go to step three. A word should be said first, though, about your private meetings. Each meeting should be followed up with a brief written summary of the essence of the meeting. A sample summary follows:

To: Mr. L. Lehrer
From: Mrs. Erin Schmidt
Date: October 22, 19____
Topic: Conference of October 20, 19____

Dear Mr. Lehrer:

Thank you for your kind attention to my concerns during our meeting of October 20. The following is a summary of my perceptions of the meeting:

1. *I asked that, should it be necessary for Cathy to miss an extracurricular activity, or should it be necessary for her to provide information about any non-school activity which interfered with a school activity, you call me for the information instead of asking Cathy about it.*

2. *You indicated to me your complete willingness to cooperate with my request. (Or, if the teacher was uncooperative, "You stated that you felt that your questions were entirely reasonable and that you were not at all in sympathy with my request. I shall therefore call you to arrange to meet with you again, at which time another parent, Mr. Tom Morelli, will accompany me.")*

3. *You asked that I contact you, ahead of time, if Cathy had to miss an activity.*

Please let me know, by return letter, if any of my recollections above are in error.

Sincerely,

Mrs. Erin Schmidt

Your sealed letter should be delivered to the school secretary who should be asked to give you a note, or to initial a prepared note, saying that the letter was delivered.

Step Three: Should the teacher be uncooperative, it is then necessary to seek the principal's intervention. Again, a *written* request, similar to the one below, should be submitted.

To: Mr. Al Fischer, Principal
Bellweather High School
From: Mrs. Erin Schmidt
Topic: Request for Intervention
Date: November 3, 19____

Dear Mr. Fischer:
Enclosed is a copy of a letter summarizing the content of a meeting between Mr. Lehrer and me, and a copy of a letter summarizing the content of a second meeting between Mr. Lehrer, Mr. Tom Morelli and me.
A solution to the problem has not been attained as of this date.

Desired Action: *I herewith request that you:*

1. *Direct Mr. Lehrer to honor his commitment to me by having him contact me personally, in writing, with a copy to you, to let me know when an extracurricular event is to be scheduled; or,*

2. *Schedule a meeting for all of us for the purpose of achieving a solution to the problem.*

3. *Please respond to this request in writing informing me of your decision.*

Sincerely,

Mrs. Erin Schmidt
cc: Mr. L. Lehrer
*   Mr. Tom Morelli*

Note that this communication provides a summary of past meetings so there is no need to repeat your complaint or to argue about what transpired. You will have either the teacher's written acknowledgment of the accuracy of your written perceptions of your meetings, or the teacher's implied acceptance of the accuracy of your perceptions if the teacher failed to correct, in writing, any of your statements. (The secretary's initials on your date of delivery preclude the teacher's claiming that he did not receive the letter.)

This communication also lets the principal know, specifically, what you requested as a response and what you expect him to do. It would be readily construed by any outside observer that it would be unreasonable of the principal not to take constructive action. With this approach, you have already begun to build an extremely solid foundation for your case should you need to go to a higher authority.

Of course, if the principal schedules a meeting, you should again provide a written summary, with appropriate copies to all participants, of your perceptions of the meeting, asking for written clarification of any misperceptions. If a serious difference of opinion is put in writing, it will be necessary to meet again and rediscuss or otherwise achieve a consensus of what actually transpired. Making a tape recording of a conference is a judicious idea, but it hinders an atmosphere which is free of threat.

Note that in the correspondence to the principal no copies were sent to his superiors. Remember that the principal has the same need to be respected, to feel unthreatened, and to have job security as the teacher does. (This is not to be confused with copying the superiors on a complimentary letter.) Bring the matter to the attention of the principal's superiors only if you have no success in resolving the situation as privately as possible.

Of course, if you solve the problem with the principal's help, you should send a letter of commendation to the superintendent telling him of the principal's outstanding professionalism in responding to your concerns. (There is no need to specify the problem here.) Your commendatory letter should then indicate, at the bottom, that you've sent a copy to the Board of Education and also to the principal. It pays to praise!

Major Barrier Number Five: Doing Your "Homework"

In recent years, the Hatch Amendment has been indiscriminately wielded by emotional parents in a frenzied attempt to control curricular content or teaching methods, often to the direct detriment of parents' rights in the public schools. A fair-minded reader will acknowledge that letters to the public schools derived from the Hatch Amendment (see Appendix A) have constituted an explicit or an implicit threat to teachers and administrators alike.

In the book of Proverbs we are told, "A gentle answer turns away wrath, but a harsh word stirs up anger" (Proverbs 15:1, NASB) and that "by forbearance a ruler may be persuaded, and a soft tongue breaks the bone" (25:15). Threats, whether actual or perceived, evoke defensive reactions. They cause the construction of barriers and the erection of obstacles against attack. For example, in response to an avalanche of Hatch Amendment-originated form letters (similar to the letter in Appendix B), "NEA Board Briefs: A Report From Colorado's Board of Directors" (May, 1985) states:

HATCH AMENDMENT:
RENEWED EFFORTS: SECOND THOUGHTS

STATE VERSIONS OF THE HATCH AMENDMENT

To anti-public school activists, the free market system seems to be a good idea everywhere but in the realm of ideas. And enemies of the free marketplace of ideas remain busy. Phyllis Schlafly and her cohorts appear to be intensifying their efforts to encourage introduction of "little Hatch Amendments" in state legislatures.

Reports from state affiliates and from People for the American Way indicate that such bills have been introduced or are expected to be introduced in seven states—California, Illinois, Arizona, Pennsylvania, North Dakota, Missouri, and North Carolina—in addition to Oklahoma, where a law similar to the Hatch Amendment has been in effect since 1981.

So far, the Department of Education reports that it has received five complaints claiming violations of the federal law. Information about the source or status of the complaints is not available.

LIMITATIONS ON THE FEDERAL LAW

The campaign for state "pupil privacy" measures may have gained new momentum now that the limited scope of the federal law has been emphasized by both its sponsor, Sen. Orrin Hatch, and the new Secretary of Education, William Bennett.

The statement by Hatch, entered into the Congressional Record on February 19, pointed out that the only school activities to which the Hatch Amendment applies are those programs, *financed by Chapter II funds, which are "experimental, demonstrational, or testing programs, the primary purpose of which is to elicit the type of information proscribed by the Hatch Amendment."* He said that some parent groups have exaggerated the scope of both the statute and the regulations interpreting them so broadly "that they would have them apply to all curriculum materials, library books, teacher guides, etc., paid for with State or local money."

Within three weeks, Secretary Bennett, echoing the law's sponsor, stated that the disputed rules do not apply to teachers' guides and instructional materials in the regular classroom.

BENNETT COMMENTS

In a statement earlier this month, Secretary Bennett even seemed to express some doubts about the Hatch Amendment. In an interview on the Christian Broadcasting Network's (CBN) 700 Club on April 8, Bennett said, "It will be a very sad day" when parents use the so-called Hatch Amendment to its furthest extent and involve the federal government in deciding whether schools should teach things of which parents disapprove. He warned against overzealousness, saying teachers should be "given room to teach" and should be allowed to act as "parents' surrogates."

But in the same interview, Bennett made it clear that his sympathies lie with the protesting groups. Asked whether teachers should ask students to write a daily journal, Bennett asked, "What about the child's right to the privacy of his own thoughts and beliefs? Why should that be probed by the teacher if the parents and the child don't want to do that?" He went on to say to the CBN audience that schools are teaching "a fair amount of inappropriate material" that parents may want removed. "I don't see why we can't take some of this inappropriate material out of the classroom . . . and get back to the things we should be teaching."

SCHLAFLY DENIES

Faced with the Hatch and Bennett clarifications, even Phyllis Schlafly has had to backtrack. In a March 1985 newsletter she denies that the famous "sample parents letter" she circulated earlier this year concerned the Hatch Amendment at all. She says:

> "It is important to note what the Sample Parents Letter IS and what it is NOT. It is a useful summary of what is wrong with public schools today . . . *The letter is NOT a list of what the Pupil Right Amendment forbids.*"

Schlafly's denial is welcome, even though after the fact. Her original mailing of the "Sample Parents Letter" made it clear that she regarded the list of 34 restricted activities within the scope of the law. The letter was introduced with a statement that it could be sent to local school boards "in order to protect parental and student rights under the Hatch Amendment." The statement informed parents that the letter "demands that the schools obey the law and secure written parental consent before subjecting the children to any of the following."

But Schlafly is not to be daunted. The limitations of the Hatch Amendment merely spur her on to widen her efforts. In her March newsletter, she says these limitations make it all the more important "to pass a Pupil Rights Amendment in every state to govern the psychological classroom methods conducted with state and local funds."

Now, does a negative or defensive response by someone with whose opinions we are at variance mean that we should not assert our rights? Not at all! In a majority of cases, however, parental influence has been resisted because of the stridency of explicit as well as implicit threats and by the nebulous nature of the complaints. So how should you voice your concerns?

The Case of the Incompetent Pastor

"We've come to get your help," the head elder of the congregation said. "We need to get rid of the pastor and we need somebody to speak for us."

"What seems to be the problem?" one of the authors of this book replied.

"He's not doing the job, that's all!" the second elder emphatically asserted.

"Well, what exactly is he not doing?" the listener queried. "How do you know he's not doing the job?"

The response was one of controlled indignation, as though the request for specifics was an affront to the elders' intelligence.

"What do you mean, how do we know he's not doing the job? We're elders, aren't we? We see the man. We can tell he's not doing the job! We want him out!"

"Well, on what basis? Has he not made enough evangelism calls?"

Again, the response was vigorous and unhesitating. "I don't know! What's that got to do with it?"

"How many evangelism calls is he supposed to make per month? Do you have any idea?"

"No..." the second elder's voice trailed off. A frown of consternation covered his face in response to the listener's

143

seemingly obstinate obtuseness. "What's your point? Why the questions?"

"Look, you guys, you say you want to get rid of the pastor—that he's not doing his job. But you haven't told me why he's not doing his job. You need to be specific. How is he not doing his job? What are your criteria? Is he making hospital visitations?"

"Well . . . yes, but . . . "

"Is he providing counseling based on the Scriptures? Is he available to help people when they call for his assistance?"

Angry frustration colored the response. "We don't know! What business is it of ours to ask people whether he gives counseling? We came here to ask you to help us get rid of the guy because he's not doing the job. Instead, you end up asking us a lot of questions, and you act like we're the ones on trial here. What are you trying to prove, anyway?"

It was now the listener's turn to get frustrated. "I can't believe you guys!" he declared incredulously. "You come here to oust a man from what he perceives is a divinely ordained call from God. You can't tell me anything about him. You don't know how many evangelism calls he makes. You don't have a clue about the content of his counseling, or for that matter, whether he's available to the people in the church. You haven't said a thing about his preaching—the content or the delivery—or how much time he spends preparing for his sermons. You haven't offered a word about his administrative ability, his level of morality—nothing! You 'just know' he isn't doing the job! Sorry, you guys, but that just doesn't cut it. The least you can do is provide specific evidence of specific failures to do the job. I can't even begin to help you state a case until I know what the problem is, and whether you've talked to the pastor about it in private."

A long-standing association between the elders and the listener kept the meeting from completely losing its cordiality, but relationships were strained as the two elders departed. They adamantly declared, in parting, that the listener just 'didn't get their point,' and that they couldn't understand why he couldn't see what they were trying to get across. They were right. The listener didn't get their point because no point was made. Instead, a blunt and nebulous allegation had been leveled. And the listener couldn't see what they were trying to get across because what was offered was a cloudy and vague abstraction that someone "wasn't doing his job." Yet both elders were well educated, and both had extremely strong feelings about the issue—so strong that ultimately it was they, rather than the pastor, who left the congregation.

Perhaps they possessed an inordinately acute level of spiritual discernment which they were unable to articulate. If so, they were certainly justified in removing themselves from the church. But they were not justified in publicly agitating the congregation by bringing a nebulous charge against the pastor.

Nor is any parent justified in bringing charges against a teacher or against the public schools without thoroughly documenting his case with specific criteria.

Making an Impact by Being Prepared

Many educators have drafted formal documents for the submission of complaints by parents so that their comments have maximum impact. These documents include questions similar to the questions on the sample form used in a Missouri public school district.

CITIZEN'S REQUEST FOR RECONSIDERATION OF A BOOK

Author _____ Hardcover _____ Paperback _____

Title _____

Publisher (if known) _____

Request initiated by _____

Telephone _____ Address _____

City _____ Zone _____

Complainant represents himself _____

(name of organization) _____

(identify other group) _____

1. To what in the book do you object? (Please be specific; cite pages)

_____

_____

_____

2. What do you feel might be the result of reading this book? _____

_____

_____

3. For what age group or course would you recommend this book?

_____

4. Is there anything good about this book? _____

_____

5. Did you read the entire book? _____ What parts? _____

_____

6. Have you read reviews of this book by literary critics? _____

_____

If so, which ones? _____

7. What do you believe is the theme or intent of this book? _____

_____

8. What would you like your school to do about this book?

_____ do not assign it to my child

_____ withdraw it from all students

_____ send it back to the review committee

9. In its place, what book of equal literary quality would you recommend that would convey as valuable a picture and perspective of our civilization? _____

_____

_____

_____

Signature of Complainant

A more detailed Reconsideration Form from a suburban school district in Colorado is reproduced on the following pages. The first part of the form requests information which is almost identical to that requested on the form used by the Missouri school district. Some of the questions appear to be directly and legitimately related to a reconsideration request, such as question number five, which implies that certain objectives might legitimately lend themselves to exploration through use of the media under challenge. Other questions, however, such as questions one through three, appear to be challengeable in terms of whether they are pertinent to the parents' ultimate concern, i.e., the appropriateness of the materials for their children. Question three, it might be inferred, is inappropriate in that it seems to imply that the source from which the criticism emanated will have a bearing upon the school district's arbitration board's response.

CITIZEN'S REQUEST FOR RECONSIDERATION OF LEARNING RESOURCES

Request initiated by _____ Date _____
Telephone _____ Address _____
School where process was initiated _____
Complainant represents:
   Individual _____ Group or Organization _____
   Please identify _____
Title of Resource _____
Type of Resource (book, film, record, speaker, other)

_____

Author _____ Publisher _____
1. Did you examine, review, or listen to this learning resource or presentation in its entirety? Yes _____ No _____
    If no, comment: _____

_____

2. Are you aware of the judgment of this resource by professional critics? Yes _____ No _____

If no, would you be interested in receiving this information? Yes _____ No _____

3. Describe what prompted your concern about this resource, such as: resource assigned to your child, resource reviewed by local or national group, other: _____
_____
_____
_____

4. In what unit of study is this resource used? _____
_____

5. Are you familiar with the School District's program objectives related to this unit of study? Yes _____ No _____

6. To what do you object concerning the presentation of this resource? Please be specific in your references (page numbers, words, scenes, illustrations, content, etc.)
_____
_____
_____
_____
_____
_____
_____

(Please attach additional information if appropriate.)

7. What do you think might be the result of exposing students to this resource? _____
_____

8. What would you like the school to do about this resource?
_____
_____
_____

9. For what age group would you recommend the presentation of this resource? _____
_____

10. What benefits, if any, do you feel could be derived from the presentation of this resource? _____
_____

11. What theme or message do you think is conveyed by the presentation of this resource? _____
_____
_____

12. Do you believe there is anything good about the resource? If so, please describe: _____
_____
_____

13. Other: _____
_____
_____

Return Completed Form to School Principal

_____
Signature of Complainant

It is probable that some districts will be even more specific, seeking documented responses; that is, specific examples of how children are being negatively affected when parents seek to change curricular content or teaching methodology. For example, in Arizona, parents Lois and Peter Morgan, upon asserting their concerns, questions, and complaints to their local school board, were asked for specific evidence to substantiate their concerns. The July 1985 *American Education Report* chronicled the Morgans' experience:

> When they presented their questions and complaints to the local school board, the response was to require answers to a list of questions, about "the nature and extent of the damage to your children," "documentation of such damage," "precisely how (i.e., the sequential, mechanistic process) the material caused . . . damage to the children." There was a list of ten such pushy and unsympathetic questions, requiring resources of specialized education and time not available to any ordinary parent. Yet further communication with the school became contingent on providing such answers.

The last line, above, is especially significant. Providing specific evidence, however, is also important for two other reasons:

1. It protects good teachers, including dedicated Christian teachers, from nebulous, generalized charges and attacks from the extreme left, from those who would seek to gag teachers from expressing traditional values or from expressing values which, while not expressly sectarian, can be clearly shown to be derived from the teachings of Jesus Christ.

2. If a case is to be built which can successfully penetrate a legal defense, the case *must* be built upon a foundation of specific evidence.

American Education Report cited Peter Morgan's frustration with the school board's demand for specificity:

"Why am I challenged and intimidated with a demand to prove these things? They are placing a burden of proof and diagnosis on me, assuming their system could not be wrong. They just reacted defensively, and nothing was done." This is said to be a common reaction to such complaints by parents.

Morgan's understandable frustration notwithstanding, it is reasonable to assume that as much evidence as possible should be amassed in substantiation of a complaint. To be effective, we must be prepared. And being prepared means being specific.

It is not enough, if we are to be effective, to object on the basis of intuition, emotion, or even self-assessed divinely-endowed spiritual insight. Undocumented, nebulous, and emotional allegations (such as those made by the church elders), do much harm to the cause of parents' rights in achieving influence in public education, no matter how strong our feelings are.

In contrast, a perfect example of the documenting of challenges to the legitimacy of the status quo is provided in the Scriptures. Consider Jesus' admonishings of the religious leaders, the educational establishment, of His day. In each case, He specified *why* they were deficient. The Apostle Paul, too, documented his criticisms, stating in his various letters specifics similar to the following:

> It is actually reported that... (I Corinthians 5:1). For I have been informed... that there are quarrels among you. Now I mean this... Each one of you is saying... (I Corinthians 1:11-12).

One of the best sources of help for parents in presenting their case should be available in the school district office. Most districts have a written statement of policy on how materials are selected. For example, a sample of excerpts from the policy of the Colorado Springs, Colorado public schools can be found in Appendix C. Selection policies often include criteria for evaluating materials, objectives for selecting materials, and procedures for parents to challenge materials.

Oftentimes, the objectives for selecting materials can tell you what the objectives of specific courses will be even though no course objectives are available. *The most effective and potent challenge to materials or to content will be one in which you as a parent can demonstrate how the district's materials or curriculum violate its own guidelines.* Districts such as the Colorado Springs Public Schools and the Ft. Wayne, Indiana Public Schools go to great lenths to obtain parental involvement in selecting materials realizing that such involvement will preclude difficulties at a later time.

Some schools in districts such as the Cherry Creek School District in Denver, Colorado conduct end-of-year surveys of parents and school personnel to obtain input into their curricula. An outstanding sample of such a survey is found in Appendix D.

Also, on the following pages you will find a "Materials/Methods Reconsideration Initiative" form. The form will help you to document your concerns about any aspect of your child's education. We suggest that you ask your district to adopt the form. The form is fair to parents, yet it is also fair to the schools who are your partners in education.

151

Materials/Methods Reconsideration Initiative

I herewith initiate a reconsideration review of the following:
- ☐ Objectives of course or unit in _____
- ☐ Printed materials
    - ☐ a. textbooks
    - ☐ b. supplementary books or periodicals
    - ☐ c. supplementary handouts, teacher-made materials, or other unpublished materials
    - ☐ d. other (specify) _____
- ☐ Non-print materials
    - ☐ a. films, filmstrips, slides or videotapes
    - ☐ b. computer programs
    - ☐ c. posters or other graphic aids
    - ☐ d. audio tapes
- ☐ Speaker(s)
- ☐ Resource person(s) or agencies
- ☐ Non-certificated support personnel
- ☐ Content of course(s), unit(s), or presentation(s)
- ☐ Quantity or type of assignments or projects
- ☐ Method(s) of instruction

The above violate(s) the district's:
- ☐ selection policies; specifically _____
- ☐ philosophy of education; specifically _____
- ☐ objectives; specifically _____

and/or

The element(s) indicated above is/are unacceptable to me in that the effects are detrimental to my child's:
- ☐ emotional well-being
- ☐ spiritual belief system; i.e., religious faith
- ☐ physical well-being
- ☐ family life and parent-child interaction
- ☐ social adjustment
- ☐ freedom of expression
- ☐ academic growth
- ☐ right to privacy in personal or family matters
- ☐ _____ (specify)

Specifically, the elements in question are detrimental to my attempts as a parent to teach appreciation of and adherence to the concepts embodied in:

☐ the Decalogue (The Ten Commandments)
☐ my interpretation of narratives or tenets in the Bible, the Koran, the Eightfold Path, the Book of Mormon or _____

_____

(specify religious source material)
☐ a Christian, Jewish, Mormon, Unitarian, Muslim, or _____
   _____ religious belief system with regard to (check one):
   ☐ a. sexual behavior
   ☐ b. family life and family relations
   ☐ c. gender identification (sex roles)
   ☐ d. religious writings
   ☐ e. civic responsibility
   ☐ f. economic stewardship
   ☐ g. conflict and conflict resolution
   ☐ h. decision-making and problem-solving
   ☐ i. international relations
   ☐ j. appropriate public decorum (social behavior)
   ☐ k. physical or spiritual health practices
   ☐ l. freedom of choice
   ☐ m. aesthetics

The element(s) under challenge will be detrimental to my child in that it/they will:
   ☐ present as acceptable alternatives one or more values, behaviors, or concepts considered, in my religious frame of reference, as so beyond the scope of acceptability or tenability that exposure would be detrimental to my child's unequivocal adherence to his spiritual upbringing.
   ☐ result in embarrassment or social ostracism or undue personal discomfort or anxiety, or effectively abridge his freedom of speech.

In the absence of the school's documented evidence that no other educational vehicles or objectives are available which would result in

153

an equivalent educational experience for my child, a reconsideration action is herewith initiated. I:

    ☐ would   ☐ would not

like to be included in identifying an alternative experience for my child.

I request a written response to this reconsideration initiative.

_____

(signed)

This form may be reproduced without written permission from the publishers if credit is given to: CLASSROOMS IN CRISIS © 1986, Accent Publications, Inc., Denver, Colorado.

If a district does not encourage the type of positive input cited above, and if the district's procedures for challenging materials are unusually difficult, you may need help from a professional educator who can help you build a good case for your complaints. Chapter 10 includes a list of organizations from which parents can get help in building such a case.

Whether you enlist the help of an outside source, use a district's already developed form, or whether you are successful in getting your administration to adopt the form on the preceding pages, the important thing to remember in registering your concerns is this: *It doesn't matter how strong your feelings are in supporting your case. What matters is how strong your case is in supporting your feelings.*

Let's assume you live in Colorado. Your child's ninth grade social studies teacher is advocating socialism over capitalism. Your child shares his school experiences with you. You go through channels, ultimately complaining to the principal that the teacher's emphasis is "un-American." You "just know" it doesn't reflect what you were taught. You will probably get nowhere with your complaint. Your appeal, although justifiable, is not documented.

If, on the other hand, your child takes newspaper editorials and other material critical of socialism and supportive of capitalism to school, with a request from you (in writing, of course) that the materials be made available to the class; and if the teacher deliberately suppresses a legitimate point of view which opposes his point of view, Colorado statute provides legal remedy. In short, you can prove that the teacher violated the law. You can be specific. You can document the fact that you complained. You have a good case; you can be sure that you will have some type of impact.

The Demand for Documentation: How Protecting the Schools Protects the Rights of Christian Clients of the Public Schools

A public school administrator who is hostile to the parents' rights movement would probably like nothing better than to have an emotional, strident, undocumented attack on the schools to display to the small segment of the community which reads letters to the editor, which votes in school bond elections, and which is otherwise active politically. The broad brush of radicalism can then be successfully used to neutralize future attempts by parents to influence their schools.

The fact cannot be emphasized enough that a parent must build a logical, rational, and documentable case. Consider, for example, the chaos which would ensue in the face of any of the following situations:

Parent "A" opposes any use of visual aids in a classroom because of the Biblical proscription pertaining to the making of "graven images," while Parent "B" demands accommodation of his hearing-impaired child's needs for all kinds of visual aids because of his abilities as a visual learner.

Parent "C" objects to boys and girls being taught in the same classroom because his religion prohibits comingling of the sexes in public places, while Parent "D," an avowed ERA advocate, objects to what he perceives to be rampant sexism in the schools, exemplified by the segregating of males and females in school team sports.

Suppose still another parent criticized a teacher's attempts to extol the virtues of patriotism as "red-necked jingoism," or "bloody-shirt chauvinism," while yet another parent espousing a world view of international affairs demanded less American history and more social studies and cited students' gross ignorance of geography in support of his position. Meanwhile, in the same classroom, suppose that three other sets of parents demanded an end to music education on the grounds that it was an expendable frill which had supplanted the basics. However, an opposing set of parents, who had no knowledge of the first set of parents' opposition to music education, demanded a greater emphasis and more time for music on the grounds that the arts and aesthetics help to enrich life and teach children to appreciate the many diverse talents beyond the mere academic ability which God has given.

In the same school district, Parent "E" emotionally demands that bi-lingual children be taught in the primary grades in their language of major fluency, while Parent "F," who was forced to learn English upon his enrollment into school as a non-English speaking student, clamors, equally as emotionally, for instruction in English as the best way to teach children to survive the academic rigor of the public schools.

Mere opinion or feeling could not support any of these positions.

Are these examples far-fetched? One of the authors remembers his experience as a principal, attempting to reason with a set of parents who demanded an end to the football, basketball and volleyball programs in a Christian school because, according to the parents, " ... the book of Revelation says that in the last days the heathen will be found chasing balls." (No Scripture reference was given.) Needless to say, the Board of Christian Education wasted no time in dismissing the complaint.

They chose to spend their time, instead, resolving conflicting criticisms by two opposing sets of parents of children in the same classroom that there was "too much memory work" and "too little memory work." The opinion that ultimately prevailed was the one which the parents supported *by documenting their case with evidence*—in this instance, the school's own set of guidelines and objectives relative to memory work.

Having an Influence Through Influencing the Community

Let's suppose that a school administration has made decisions which are perfectly legal but which are very unpopular. If the response from the community is one of silence, the school administration will make no changes. Suppose, though, that parents organize for action. They shape public opposition. It is not likely that school administrators would pursue a course of action which results in a barrage of visits to classrooms by angry parents, or a mass of confrontative conferences at school, or criticism and widespread, negative publicity.

There are a variety of reasons why this is so. First, school officials are people, too. Nobody enjoys the glaring spotlight of public criticism. Second, most professionals aspire to higher achievement in their profession. Few administrators want to carry to their next job application the fact of community dissatisfaction with their leadership. But the most important reason why administrators will be responsive to their various publics is a financial one. Where funding issues are put to a vote of the community, public school administrators can ill afford to alienate the voters. Indeed, this fact is readily acknowledged by educators themselves, as the following advice in *Social Education, the Official Journal of the National Council for the Social Studies,* clearly demonstrates:

> The public has a right to know what kind of education takes place in public schools and a right to voice concern about the textbook used . . . . We tended to accuse textbooks protesters of attempting to engage in censorship when they were simply trying very hard to win support for some ideas that we strongly opposed . . . . The day when we begin to regard any part of our public as the enemy, we have begun a pattern of behavior that we will come to regret. [1]

One organization which has been acutely sensitive to the value of influencing the community is People for the American Way. This organization perceives a threat to quality education emanating from, primarily, the Far Right. It's possible that People for the American Way might label the authors of this book, each of whom is a Christian, a part of the Far Right. Nevertheless, credit must be given where credit is due. Therefore, it is desirable to point out that some materials produced by People for the American Way can be very useful in advancing the cause of parents' rights in the public schools, including the cause of conservative Christian parents.

In response to the threat they perceive, the organization has published a book entitled, *Protecting the Freedom to Learn: A Citizen's Guide.* Although a substantial number of the opinions and objectives presented in the book, as well as the tenor of parts of the book, would be anathema to many Christians, the suggestions delineated under the heading "Organizing in Your Community" are excellent. The tactics, ideas, and actions suggested are well written, legal, and potentially effective. They can be profitably employed by *any* group striving to have an influence upon the public schools. Selected excerpts from the book are reproduced here by permission.

ORGANIZING IN YOUR COMMUNITY

3. Circulating Petitions

Like letter writing, a neighborhood petition drive can help to educate your community and to influence decision makers. A bonus: A petition drive also can help organize the community and attract media attention. Whether or not you choose to start a petition drive will depend on the amount of time you have, the number of willing volunteers, and your assessment of potential for success. So if you decide a petition drive is appropriate for your community and situation, here are a few suggestions.

Planning Your Strategy: If possible, before starting your petition drive, plan a target date for the presentation of your petitions. If there isn't an important date that ties in with the drive—such as a school board meeting where your specific issue will be discussed—you should establish a tentative time frame for the campaign. A drive that goes on too long may become tiresome and lose its effectiveness. Establish the goals of the drive and determine approximately how many signatures you'll need to "be successful." If the issue is hot enough in your community and you feel 100 percent confident of success, you might want to alert the press to your activities or even invite them to a "kick off" meeting or rally.

Writing Your Petition: Keep it well-focused, short, declarative, action-oriented and aimed at a specific audience. Identify the sponsoring organization and include information on where to send completed petitions. Don't threaten, make personal attacks, alienate an entire constituency of potential signers, or be shrill. See People for the American Way's petition to the Doubleday Publishing Company protesting the precensorship of "controversial material" as an example.

Circulating Your Petition: Be sure to get the greatest number of volunteers possible for the widest possible circulation. The number of places to get signatures is endless: community meetings, shopping malls, fairs or church bazaars, door-to-door in neighborhoods or apartment complexes, outside movie theaters, in laundromats, at bowling alleys, bus stops, parking lots or *any* place where people in your community gather.

Don't count on people to read even the shortest message; start conversations and explain, in a personal and friendly way, why you're circulating this petition and what their signatures will help you accomplish. Enlist the help of the most enthusiastic signers by having a supply of blank petitions that they can circulate for you.

Presenting Your Petitions: Use the size of your success to determine the size of the splash you want to make in concluding your petition drive. If things didn't go as well as hoped, you may want to present your signatures to the school board president during office hours. If things went well, you may want to present them at a packed board meeting full of reporters and news cameras.

When you're successful, don't be afraid to draw attention to your success in preparation for the fight that's still ahead.

4. Working with the Media

Press coverage can be a valuable tool in your attempts to block censorship in your community. Alerting the press to the threats that censors pose to the freedom to learn can help you alert supporters you didn't know you had. Good press coverage of your concerns can influence the decision makers as well as those in the community who share your concern. Favorable media attention also can help to create a climate in which solutions are easier to find and apply.

Sometimes television and radio stations and newspapers can be imposing institutions, but remember: They're made up of people whose job it is to package and sell news to your community. Often, they're overworked, short-handed and hassled, which means that sometimes they're too busy to seek out an interesting—and important—local story such as the one you have to offer. Your task is to let the media know—succinctly—that an unfolding censorship story ultimately will be a story that affects and interests the majority of the community. Your best bet is to approach the media with confidence as a responsible member of your community. Your concerns are news. When properly presented, they should be of interest to broadcast audiences and readers of the press—your community.

Here are a few pointers on how to get the media interested in threats to your children's education.

How to Contact the Press

● *First, work up a good list of area press people.* Include city editors at daily and weekly area newspapers, assignment editors at local radio and TV stations, and the statewide Associated Press and United Press International bureaus (usually located in the state capitals). Call ahead to get the names and titles of those reporters and editors who usually cover education issues; an envelope addressed to Ms. Betty Smith may be opened days before the one addressed simply to "City Editor."

● *Next, you may want to prepare a news release.* A release can announce an important meeting, advise the press that crucial decisions are expected soon, make a statement, or publicize an event, such as the official formation of a new, pro-public education group. The lead paragraph should always include who, what, where, when and why. Your organization's point of view should be expressed in quotations from your spokesperson. Other tips: Your press release should be typed, double spaced, no longer than one or two pages, and include a spokesperson's name and number so the press know whom to call with questions.

● *Finally, and most important, you should call your media contacts on a regular basis* to be assured of successful news coverage. Calls can be made to alert the press to fast-breaking news, to make a statement commenting on a timely news story, to follow up news release as a reminder that you'll be making news at the next night's school board meeting, or to let the reporters who missed a meeting know what they missed.

What to Say: There are several points pertaining to nearly all attacks against the public schools that we should be repeating over and over again—especially to reporters. Here are a few to put on your internal tape recorder for play back at every possible opportunity:

● "Those people trying to (select one: remove books from our shelves/rewrite history/teach religion in science classes/eliminate sex and drug education from our schools) have every right to state their opinions, and in fact, we welcome their doing so. Parental input is an important part of quality public education. But let's not confuse local control with vocal control. We don't want a small minority—no matter how loud—dictating what all of our children learn, or don't learn."

● "This is not just an isolated incident happening here on Main Street, U.S.A. It's part of a national anti-public education movement—involving Phyllis Schlafly's Eagle Forum, the Pro-Family Forum, the

Gabler's Educational Research Analysts and the Moral Majority—that would like to indoctrinate students to their narrow religious and philosophical point of view. I'd be glad to show you their literature, tell you who wrote it, and give you information about when and where it's been distributed before."

● "While we're all concerned about this (select one: book, curriculum, film, principle), we should remember that this is not just an issue of censorship. It's an issue of our children's right to learn in public, tax-supported schools. The censorship movement is really an organized all-out attack against public schools. We're here, in part, to protect the institution of public education."

How to Say It: How your point of view is described by the media depends on two things: your credibility and—most important with the electronic press—your image.

Establishing credibility with the media takes time and effort. Here are a few suggestions:

● Only call or write the press when you have news to report—don't pester them with asides or peripheral matters. When you call, you want them to know it's important.

● Have your facts and all supporting evidence in front of you when talking with the press. If you don't know an answer, say so. Get the information and call back.

● Be persistent but not a pest. Keep reminder calls brief, but feel free to make them. Don't write off a reporter or editor just because he or she doesn't seem interested at first. Keep trying, but always remain friendly.

● Never make personal attacks against members of the press or against those who oppose your point of view. If an attack is made against your group, do not feel compelled to respond. In the midst of a lot of name-calling, your issue can get cold.

As many an advertiser has said, *your image* is as important as your product. In your dealings with the press, be conscious of the following few points:

● As often as possible, appoint or elect one spokesperson. More than one will confuse the press and the public.

● Always make it clear whom that spokesperson represents. If you've organized a pro-public education group that includes members of the local clergy, community leaders, parents, teachers and others, say so.

If you can show the diversity of your group for the electronic press, do it.

● Any written materials you produce are likely to get a lot of attention; be conscious of the tone and image they present. Strive for an easy-to-read, simple publication. Be professional but not slick.

● Always remember that you are dealing with two branches of the press—the print shop and the electronic press. TV reporters are unlikely to cover a story unless it makes good film, so the setting and location of events and announcements can be very important. Don't be afraid to be dramatic and creative.

Finally, always keep press coverage in perspective: A good story won't win your battle for you, a bad one won't mean you've lost. One key to protecting our children's right to learn will always be organization; a common sense press strategy is only one piece of that puzzle.

5. Educating the Public

A successful campaign to protect the freedom to learn involves a strong defense and a strong offense. When you're not in the middle of a battle against local censors, you can still work to educate your community about important public education issues. Here's how:

Get on local radio and TV talk shows. Area talk show producers—especially for radio—are looking for knowledgeable guests on subjects involving local or national controversy. If you have the time, this is a media opportunity worth pursuing.

First, get a list of all such local shows, their hosts and producers. Send an introductory letter to each producer, explaining the nature of your group and the issues you would like a chance to discuss. A week or so after your mailing goes out, call each producer and discuss an appearance, even if it's weeks or months in advance. Stress the timeliness of the issues, their national importance and their local appeal to so many members of your community. Some producers may be interested in hosting a national censorship or public education expert; have them give People for the American Way's Washington office a call.

Finally, whatever the producer's initial inclination, give it your best sales pitch. If you're not successful at first, keep trying.

Write letters to the editor. Whenever timely, write letters to your local newspapers on public education issues. Short, well written letters usually have a good chance of being printed and are a good way to remind your community of the issues your group is concerned about.

Set up meetings with local groups to discuss education issues—and publicize them. Keep spreading the word by setting up meetings with school groups, church groups, local charity groups, and community groups. Arrange for speakers on important education issues. Show People for the American Way's film, "Life and Liberty . . . For All Who Believe," then discuss its relevance to the situation in your community.

But whatever the program, use the media to advertise it. Use free calendars in local papers, call radio stations to find out how to submit public service announcements about your event, and call reporters who may be especially interested in attending.

It's been People for the American Way's experience that censors and public education critics in communities around the country *never go away*. So, keep building local support by working with the media; it'll make the next battle a lot easier.

The strategies and tactics employed by People For The American Way are well thought out. They can be used, with minor changes, by any agency seeking to wield influence in the public schools. They are moral. They are legal. And they are effective. Add to their approach your knowledge, and your influence will be effective indeed. You will be armed with the knowledge of the mindset of your opponents!

Pray for Your Schools

One action for improving any situation is fervent prayer. Too often Christians exhaust every practical avenue of action they perceive, and when they experience failure they then conclude that "all I can do now is pray." This is an astounding statement considering the astonishing results of prayer recorded by the

Apostle James. It is both an admonition and encouragement to Christians everywhere:

Therefore, confess your sins to one another, and pray for one another, so that you may be healed. The effective prayer of a righteous man can accomplish much. Elijah was a man with a nature like ours, and he prayed earnestly that it might not rain; and it did not rain on the earth for three years and six months. And he prayed again, and the sky poured rain, and the earth produced its fruit (James 5:16-18, NASB).

How to Become a Decision-Maker in Your Schools

One of the most effective ways to have an influence in your schools is to become actively involved in its decision-making processes. Research conducted for this book revealed that the level of parental involvement encouraged by specific schools or specific districts varies tremendously from district to district, usually in response to the school officials' assessment of parental interest. Some districts have formal statements explaining how parents can become involved, including a description of various committees and organizations which are active in the particular district or in individual schools. Some districts allow individual schools to form their own parent committees for specific purposes identified by the principals, parents and teachers of those schools. Because the level of parental involvement provided for varies so greatly from district to district, the following procedure for determining action in your area is suggested:

1. Call your child's school and ask for a copy of material which describes how parents can become involved. You will either:
   a. Receive the material;
   b. Be apprised that no such material is available;
   c. Be directed to call the district office for the material;
   d. Be asked by a puzzled and bemused administrator "what you mean," in which case it will be necessary for you to explain your desire to be of assistance to the

school and to the school district by being actively involved in parent-teacher or parent-administrator committees.

2. If the school or the district has no such committee, you then have a golden opportunity to find other capable people who, like you, have an interest in influencing their schools. Ask them to go with you to the school principal or to the superintendent to suggest forming committees on which parents can serve. Some extremely impact-creating committees to serve on or create are:

   a. *School Accountability Council* - The Colorado Springs, Colorado brochure on School Accountability Councils—what they are, what they do and how to get involved in them—is an excellent example of good school-community communication. The brochure is reproduced in Appendix E.

   b. *Materials Selection Committee* - The Colorado Springs public schools have an exemplary comprehensive process of materials selection mentioned earlier which has been, in part, reproduced in Appendix C. The process provides for maximal input from the public.

   c. *Teacher Evaluation Committee*

   d. *Teacher Selection Committee*

   e. *Parents' Advisory Council*

In one school, the Parents' Advisory Council was the final arbiter in a dispute between parents at a school fund-raising Book Fair. Several Christian parents had objected to other parents' offering the game Dungeons and Dragons for sale at the Book Fair. The parents agreed to abide by the parent council's decision. The result? The game was offered for sale, but children were not allowed to examine or purchase it without their parents being actively involved in both the examination and the purchase. Was the outcome completely satisfactory to the Christian parents? No, but it honored their concerns and also addressed the legitimate desires of the other parents.

There probably would have been no legal remedy which

would have favored the Christian parents, and other remedies pursued with strident demands and emotional, undocumented opinions would have hurt the cause of "holding out the Word of Life" far more than the presence of an admittedly undesirable "game."

Less formal but still effective committees can be created independent of the schools. For example, an independent "Excellence in Education" committee can host "Teacher Appreciation" breakfasts or other events. Such a committee can also take out newspaper ads to recognize a "Teacher of the Month," or "School of the Month." In addition, independent committees can provide support and assistance to teachers, especially Christian teachers, who come under attack from the far right or the far left—however those terms may be defined.

It is vital to remember that you need not be left without a voice in the administration of your public schools. You can, of course, run for public office. Most public school administrators welcome parental input because greater parental involvement ultimately translates into better working conditions, better salaries, and better morale for public school personnel through the support of public school funding measures. If the school system in which you find yourself has a well-developed parent involvement program, the doors are wide open for your influence to be asserted. The Cherry Creek School District of suburban Denver, Colorado is one of many school districts with an exemplary record of encouraging parental input in the educative process. Appendix F includes a copy of a letter sent by the Parents' Council which is indicative both of the level and the nature of school-community cooperation which can be attained.

If there are no organizations, create them, staff them, and use them to shape the direction of your schools! There can be no control of the schools by "globalists," "one-worlders," "Secular Humanists," or any other spectre of malevolence if Christian parents dominate the membershp of committees with the sheer force of numbers or the sheer power of informed opinion.

Chapter 9

Legal Issues: How To Get Counsel

Classroom Crisis #1: Your child's school sponsors a dance every Friday night. The proceeds help pay for needed improvements at school. To bolster attendance, the principal announces that attendance is required for all students. The problem is, your convictions forbid dancing, and you don't want your children present where dancing is the main activity. You exhaust the usual avenues of conciliation and the principal still demands your child's attendance. You could go into the principal's office, scream your head off, and end up with a major crisis in which everybody loses, especially your child. But, instead, you hire an attorney. The attorney writes a polite but firm letter to the principal, explaining your religious objections and your First and Fourteenth Amendment rights. Either because he recognizes the merit of your position or just because he wants to avoid the expense and publicity of a lawsuit, the principal promptly grants your child an exemption from the requirement. The lawyer has saved the day.

Classroom Crisis #2: Your child's social studies teacher assigns a book that you find objectionable. You hire an attorney who writes a letter to the teachers, copies to the principal and school board, threatening lawsuits if the teacher doesn't back down immediately. The teacher is not really a bad sort of guy. Had a parent approached him tactfully and explained the problem in a polite conversation, he might readily have agreed to let your child read a different book. But the letter from the attorney has raised his hackles and he feels his rights as a teacher have been threatened. So he digs in his heels and makes a major case out of it, at thousands of dollars of legal costs to you and much emotional trauma for your child. The lawyer has created a gigantic mess that benefits no one but himself!

Lawyers can be a tremendous help or a tremendous hassle. Whether he solves your problem or makes it worse depends on the nature of your problem, what lawyer you pick, and how you work with him.

Do You Need a Lawyer?

Not every legal question requires a lawyer to answer it. To know the maximum speed the law allows on an interstate highway, you don't have to ask a lawyer; you can read the traffic signs yourself. To determine whether a lawyer is needed, you have to consider the cost of a lawyer (C) and your ability to pay (A). Then you consider the risk involved (R), and the need for a lawyer (N). Thus you arrive at a formula for determining the need for a lawyer: $C+A = R+N$. A person might be well-advised to represent himself on a speeding ticket where a $25 fine might not justify $500 for a lawyer, but representing yourself on a capital murder charge is just plain foolish!

If you simply need to talk with school officials and work out a problem, you might be able to do that by yourself. In fact, the presence of a lawyer might complicate the issue and cause both sides to become inflexible and antagonistic. On the other hand, meeting with school officials without your lawyer present can be risky because you might make statements that could be damaging to your position later.

If you need to know what the law says, you might be able to research it for yourself. If there is a law school nearby, the law librarian will probably assist you in finding what you need. Most county and federal courthouses have a law library.

Public libraries and university libraries will probably have some of the basic documents you need, such as the municipal code (city ordinances), state statutes, and the United States Code. The annotated codes are more helpful because after each statute they contain brief summaries of court cases that have interpreted that statute. If you need copies of certain federal or state regulations, you might write to those agencies and ask them to supply them. In most instances they are required by law to do so, though they might charge you a reasonable fee.

There is much you can do on your own. But if you are not certain whether you need a lawyer, it is best to retain one. Even if he does not represent you in court, he might give you helpful advice.

Finding a Lawyer

Despite the supposed overabundance of lawyers today, many people have difficulty finding a lawyer who is willing and able to help them. And, merely finding a lawyer is not enough. You need a lawyer who is "right" for you and your case. The best tax lawyer in the nation might have no understanding of or interest in constitutional cases, and a topgrade personal injury lawyer might be as out-of-place in a school case as a podiatrist trying to perform brain surgery!

The quickest place to find a lawyer is in the yellow pages of the telephone book. This, however, tells you very little about the lawyer except his name, address and telephone number. You need more than that.

The local bar association may maintain a lawyer referral service, but, again, this is of limited value. Often the bar referral service merely lists the lawyers in alphabetical order and refers each caller to the next one on the list to make sure all lawyers get equal referrals. However, some bar associations may have the attorneys indicate areas of special interest and this would be of greater help.

In many law libraries you will find a multi-volume directory of lawyers called the *Martindale-Hubbell Law Directory*. This lists lawyers according to their states and local communities. At the beginning of each volume every lawyer is listed, and in the rest of the volume space and more information is given to those attorneys whose firms have paid a substantial sum to have their names listed in this directory. The directory will tell you where the lawyer was born, where he attended school, his professional associations, representative clients, types of cases handled, published works, offices held, etc. However, the fact that a firm is given an extended listing in *Martindale-Hubbell* does not necessarily mean it is a good firm; it only means the firm has paid for an extended listing.

Martindale-Hubbell also rates the lawyers in its directory based on confidential evaluations by judges and other attorneys in the area. The lawyer's ability is rated as "A" (very high), "B" (high), or "C" (fair). However, no attorney can receive a "B" rating unless he has practiced law at least five years, nor can he receive an "A" rating until he has practiced for ten years. The best lawyer gets only a "C" if he has practiced less than five years. Lawyers are also rated on adherence to ethical standards: "V" indicates faithful adherence. But many attorneys are not rated at all, either at their own request or because the publisher does not have adequate information. These ratings are of some value but must not be regarded as conclusive.

One of the best sources of legal help is word of mouth. Perhaps your relatives have a lawyer who knows the family and its legal history. He may be able to help you or suggest someone who can. Usually, at least in smaller communities, the businessmen know which lawyers are successful and respected. Perhaps a businessman in your church could suggest a lawyer for you.

Must your lawyer be a Christian? Not necessarily. A non-Christian lawyer may be just as capable and honest as a Christian lawyer. But a Christian lawyer may understand and empathize with your problem more than a non-Christian, especially if your problem involves religious liberty.

If you cannot afford an attorney, legal aid societies may be able to help you without charge or at a reduced rate. Federally funded legal aid societies exist in many communities, and many law schools operate legal clinics as a public service and as a means of giving their students practical experience. You might look in the yellow pages under *attorneys* or *lawyers* to find legal aid or a legal clinic; or, you could call the local bar association or the social services to find out how to reach a legal aid society.

Other Sources of Help

Several Christian organizations provide legal help for Christians in cases that involve religious liberty. The Christian Legal Society is especially interested in cases involving the right of Christians to express themselves in public schools and other public facilities. The Center for Law and Religious Freedom, an arm of CLS with offices at P.O. Box 1492, 6901 Braddock Rd., Springfield, Virginia 22151, keeps a file of legal briefs and other materials which they supply to lawyers in First Amendment cases. Another CLS arm, the Christian Conciliation Service, works to reconcile disputes between Christians without going to court, and may be reached through the Oak Park office. The nationwide CLS membership list can be most helpful in locating a Christian lawyer.

Another outstanding organization is the National Legal Foundation (formerly known as the Freedom Council Foundation), 825 Greenbrier Circle, Chesapeake, Virginia 23320. (804) 424-4242. Established as part of Pat Robertson's Christian Broadcasting Network ministries, the Freedom Council Foundation actively assists in many cases involving Christian freedom. They have come to the aid of a teacher whose principal reprimanded her for reading her Bible in the teachers' lounge during lunch break; they have helped a student who was told she could not refer to Jesus Christ during her valedictory address; they have helped students whose teachers have forced them to read objectionable books; and many others.

The Rutherford Institute, P.O. Box 510, Manassas, Virginia 22110 was established by John Whitehead. The Rutherford Institute aggressively defends Christian schools and home schools, and actively fights abortion. It has also come to the aid of public school students, including a student who was denied the right to distribute anti-abortion literature at her public high school.

Concerned Women for America, founded by Beverly LaHaye, has a legal staff that is eager to assist Christians. They are currently assisting a blind student in the State of Washington whose student aid was cut off because he wants to attend theology school and the state has decided that aid for theology studies violates their concept of separation of church and state. The lawyers for CWA can be reached at 122 "C" St. N.W., Suite 800, Washington, D.C. 20001.

The National Institute for Christian Law and Education, 5310 E. 31st St., Tulsa, Oklahoma 74136 was established in 1983. Funded in part by Oral Roberts University's Educational Fellowship, the Foundation is willing to defend the rights of Christians in public, private and home schools.

The National Civil Liberties Legal Foundation, N88 W 16783 Main St., Menomonee Falls, Wisconsin 53051 was recently founded to defend the legal rights of Christians and conservatives. Under the able leadership of Christian attorneys John McLario and Wendell Bird, this group recently defeated a vigorous challenge by the American Civil Liberties Union.

The Creation-Science Legal Defense Fund, P.O. Box 78312 Shreveport, Louisiana 71137 is defending the Louisiana law which provides balanced treatment of origins in public school classrooms. The Fund may be willing to assist others who suffer discrimination because of their creationist beliefs.

The Catholic League for Religious and Civil Rights, 1100 West Wells Street, Milwaukee, Wisconsin 53233 zealously defends the religious rights of Roman Catholics and may be willing to consider other cases as well.

The Christian Law Association, 6929 W. 130th St., Suite 600, Cleveland, Ohio 44130 vigorously defends Christian schools against oppressive state regulation. While normally they represent private schools, they might defend Christians in a public school setting also.

Finally, one might turn to the American Civil Liberties Union or the Americans United for Separation of Church and State. While we strongly disagree with the radical separationist stance taken by these two groups in church-state matters (particularly the ACLU), they might be of assistance in some cases.

This is not necessarily a complete listing of all sources of legal help for Christians. The inclusion of the above organizations does not necessarily imply an endorsement of them, nor should any negative inferences be drawn from any omissions.

Working With a Lawyer

If you handle it right, working with your lawyer can be a pleasant experience.

First, discuss financial arrangements at the beginning. Expect to pay your attorney for his services unless he agrees otherwise. He sells his time and knowledge just as a grocer sells groceries, and it is amazing that Christians who would never think of asking a Christian grocer for free groceries have no qualms about asking for free legal advice from a Christian lawyer. He has tremendous overhead in his office, and normally he can't work for free. Most lawyers estimate that it costs them about $40 per hour just to meet their expenses, and only above that can they begin to make a profit. If your lawyer doesn't tell you right away, ask!

Lawyers usually charge their clients in one of three basic ways: (1) *By the hour:* this is normal for most civil defense work and for routine office work; (2)*By the job:* many lawyers have a flat rate for wills, another flat rate for reading an abstract, another for preparing a deed regardless of time involved; (3) *The contingent fee:* the lawyer receives a percentage of the amount won in the lawsuit. Obviously, the contingent fee applies only to civil lawsuits by plaintiffs. The contingent fee has come under much criticism lately, but it is the only means by which many low-income plaintiffs can afford to bring their cases to court and seek justice. Also, it is an incentive for the lawyer to work hard and do a good job because if his client doesn't win anything, he doesn't win anything, either.

In addition to the fee for his services, a lawyer normally charges you for his expenses—mileage, court filing fees, long distance telephone calls, witness fees and so on. Often he will ask for these expenses in advance. He may also expect a retainer or down payment for his services. You should expect to pay this, but you should also clarify in advance whether the unused portion of the retainer is refundable if the case ends up taking less time and expense than expected.

It is always advisable to enter into a written fee agreement with your lawyer and to keep a copy for yourself. Most lawyers insist on this and make it routine office procedure. You need to remember, however, that your lawyer probably doesn't know exactly how much the case is going to cost because he doesn't know how much time it is going to take. He doesn't know whether the other side will settle easily, or with much difficulty, or at all. He doesn't know whether the case will be settled before trial, at trial, or whether it will have to be appealed to higher courts. While fee agreements can tell you the method by which you will be charged, they usually cannot guarantee the exact amount.

One final note regarding fees: Don't select a lawyer simply because he is the least expensive. Nor should you assume a lawyer is the best because he is the most expensive. He may be expensive because he is highly skilled in some fields of law, but not necessarily yours. One lawyer may charge $50 per hour, another may charge $100. But if the $100 lawyer has handled your type of case before, he may be able to do a much better job in less than half the time and end up saving you money.

Once you find an attorney, don't just walk in on him. Unless he tells you otherwise, make an appointment to see him. He may be busy working on another case that has to be tried tomorrow morning, and even if he agrees to see you, he will resent the intrusion.

Feel free to discuss your case with your lawyer's secretary or legal assistants. If they ask you questions, they are not being nosey. They want to elicit information so they can help the lawyer get ready to see you by bringing him the right file and other materials. His secretaries and legal assistants work for much less than he does, so by utilizing them he saves you money.

When you come to see an attorney, bring all relevant paperwork with you. Failure to do so may result in a trip home, a second appointment, and possibly incomplete or incorrect legal advice.

Tell your attorney the entire story, including those elements unfavorable or embarrassing to you. It is much better that your attorney find these things out in his office so that he can prepare to counter them, than that he be surprised by them in court! The lawyer-client privilege requires that he not disclose information you have given him in confidence without your consent, unless you have perpetrated a fraud upon the court or intend to commit a serious crime.

You will need to communicate with your lawyer from time to time, but don't badger him constantly about your case. Remember that he has dozens, perhaps hundreds, of active files and can't think about your case every minute. If he hasn't called you, it may be that he has nothing to report. Perhaps he hasn't called you because the opposing attorney hasn't called him, and maybe the opposing attorney hasn't heard back from his client. Your lawyer has to charge you for his time, and if he doesn't call or write you every day, it may be that he is trying to save you money.

Also, you should not call your lawyer at his home unless he tells you to do so. Most lawyers work much more than an eight hour day and they value their time with their families. Some clients assume they shouldn't have to pay for legal services if they call or visit their lawyer at home. But treat him with the professional and Christian respect you would want for yourself.

If you are dissatisfied with your lawyer's service, you may

want to change attorneys. But it may also be that you and your lawyer haven't communicated properly, and you don't understand what he is doing for you and why he is doing it. He may be doing much more than you realize. Before changing lawyers, make an appointment, state your concern frankly, and give him an opportunity to explain. After the meeting your confidence may be restored, or you may both agree that you should change lawyers. He may be a good attorney, but not the right one for you.

If you believe your attorney has handled your case in an incompetent, unprofessional, or unethical manner, you may wish to complain to the grievance committee of the local bar association. Most bar associations are concerned about their public image and probably police the legal profession better than do most other professions. The bar association might require the attorney to perform extra services for his client or refund his legal fees, go through extra legal training to overcome deficiencies, get professional help, be reprimanded, or as a most extreme measure, temporary or permanent suspension or revocation of the right to practice law. Very few lawyer/client relationships ever end up this way, however. Most people seem to be highly satisfied with their own personal attorney.

By following the suggestions in this chapter, your attorney/client relationship can be an enjoyable and worthwhile experience for both of you.

Chapter 10

Staying Informed: Other Books

The Christian Legal Advisor by John Eidsmoe (Milford, Michigan: Mott Media, 1984) is a comprehensive reference work of legal information of special value to Christians. The book features a chapter on public schools, another on private schools, still another on home schools, and chapters on humanism and the creation/evolution controversy, all of which should be of special interest to those who are concerned about education.

God and Caesar: Christian Faith and Political Action by John Eidsmoe (Westchester, Illinois: Crossway Books, 1984) is an exegesis of a conservative Biblical position on the nature and function of government, the duty of the Christian toward government, and a Biblical position on such issues as abortion, economics, crime, and national defense. Readers might be especially interested in the chapter on education.

Schools: They Haven't Got a Prayer, by Lynn R. Buzzard (Elgin, Illinois: David C. Cook Publishing Co., 1982) is an excellent analysis of the school prayer issue. Buzzard is a past executive director of the Christian Legal Society and now a law professor at Campbell University.

The Christian Teacher and the Public Schools, by Christopher Hall (Oak Park, Illinois: Christian Legal Society, 1975, 1978 Supplement by John W. Whitehead) is a good, concise and well-organized discussion of First Amendment issues as they relate to public schools. It is written from the standpoint of teachers but its insights are valuable for parents as well.

Parents' Rights by John W. Whitehead (Westchester, Illinois: Crossway Books, 1985) covers a wide variety of topics relating to parental rights, including children's liberation, child abuse charges and public school matters.

The Supreme Court and Public Prayer by Charles E. Rice (New York: Fordham University Press, 1964) is an excellent discussion of the school prayer issue from a legal and historical perspective. Rice is a highly respected law professor at Notre Dame University.

"Freedom of Religion and Science Instruction in Public Schools," by Wendell R. Bird, *Yale Law Journal*, Vol. 87, No. 3 (January 1978) is an excellent discussion of the creation/evolution controversy. Bird, a creationist attorney, is a former editor of the *Yale Law Journal*.

The Battle for Religious Liberty by Lynn R. Buzzard and Samuel E. Ericsson (Elgin, Illinois: David C. Cook, 1982) is a good general summary of First Amendment religious liberty issues written from a Christian standpoint.

The Religious Freedom Reporter, published monthly by the Center for Law and Religious Freedom, a subsidiary of the Christian Legal Society, is the best, most complete, and most current summary of the present status of First Amendment litigation nationwide. It covers a wide variety of subjects, including education, and may be ordered through the Center at P.O. Box 1492, 6901 Braddock Road, Springfield, Virginia 22151, (703) 941-3192.

"The Establishment of the Religion of Secular Humanism and its First Amendment Implications," John W. Whitehead and John Conlan, *Texas Tech Law Review*, Vol. 10, 1978, is an excellent discussion of the meaning and implications of Secular Humanism, including but not limited to its public school context.

School Law by Kern Alexander (St. Paul, Minnesota: West Publishing Company, 1980) is an excellent casebook on legal issues in education.

The Constitution and American Education, Second Edition by Arval

A. Morris (St. Paul, Minnesota: West Publishing Co., 1980) is also a good general textbook on education law. The same could be said for *The Law of Public Education, Second Edition* by E. Edmond Reutter, Jr., and Robert R. Hamilton (Mineola, New York: Foundation Press, 1976); and *State, School and Family, Second Edition* by Michael S. Sorgen, William A. Kaplin, Patrick S. Duffy, and Ephraim Margolin (New York: Matthew Bender, 1979).

The Christian Legal Society has published an eight page pamphlet entitled "Equal Access IS the Law," a good, short, practical summary of the Equal Access Act complete with practical guidelines as to how to implement it. It is available through the Society at P.O. Box 2069, Oak Park, Illinois 60303, (312) 848-7735.

Two excellent books that explain how to evaluate your child's textbooks are *Textbooks on Trial* by James. C. Hefley (Wheaton, Illinois: Victory Books, 1976, 1977) which is the story of Mel and Norma Gabler's battle against anti-Christian textbooks; and *What Are They Teaching Our Children?* by Mel and Norma Gabler with James C. Hefley (Wheaton, Illinois: Victor Books, 1985).

The value of parental involvement in education is well articulated by Dr. and Mrs. Raymond Moore in *Home Grown Kids* (1981), *Home Spun Schools* (1982), and *Home Style Teachers* (1984), all published by Word Books of Waco, Texas; and *School Can Wait* (Washougal, Washington: Hewitt, 1979) and *Better Late than Early* (New York: Reader's Digest—Hewitt, 1976). Dr. and Mrs. Moore's monthly newsletter, *The Parent Educator and Family Report* can be ordered through the Hewitt Research Foundation, P.O. Box 9, Washougal, Washington 98671-0009.

Who Owns the Children? Compulsory Education and the Dilemma of Ultimate Authority by Blair Adams and Joel Stein (Grand Junction, Colorado: Truth Forum, 1984) is a good discussion of the controversy concerning state authority in education, written from the standpoint of those who favor parental rights.

Samuel Blumenfeld has written a hard-hitting expose of the National Education Association and its activities. It is titled *NEA: The Trojan Horse in American Education* (Boise, Idaho: Paradigm,

1984). And Phyllis Schlafly has prepared a documentary entitled *Child Abuse in the Classroom* (Westchester, Illinois: Crossway, 1984) that provides good ammunition for those who wish to fight against invasions of privacy and other abuses in the public schools.

The Christian parent who wants to stay informed on recent development in public schools might also pay close attention to contemporary Christian publications such as *Christianity Today, Christian Life, Good News Broadcaster, Moody Monthly, Christian News,* and others. These frequently contain news items of concern to Christians regarding public as well as private education.

References

Chapter 3

Creationist Materials
1. The Bible-Science Association, P.O. Box 6163, 2911 E. 42nd St., Minneapolis, MN 55406
2. Creation-Science Research Center, P.O. Box 23195, San Diego, CA 92123
3. *Biology: A Search for Order in Complexity* by John N. Moore and Harold S. Slusher (Grand Rapids: Zondervan, 1970, 1977).
4. *Evolution: The Fossils Say No!* by Duane Gish (San Diego: Creation-Life Publishers, 1978).
5. *The Biblical Flood and the Ice Epoch* by Donald Wesley Patton (Seattle: Pacific Meridian Publishing Co., 1966, 1973)
6. *The Genesis Flood* by John C. Whitcomb and Henry Morris (Philadelphia: Presbyterian and Reformed Publishing Co., 1961).
7. *The Flood in the Light of the Bible, Geology and Archeology* by Alfred M. Rehwinkel (St. Louis: Concordia, 1951).

Chapter 4

1. Roberto P. Martin, "Values Clarification: The State of the Art for the 1980s," *Innovations in Education: Reformers and Their Critics*, 4th Edition, Ed. John Martin Rich (Boston: Allyn and Bacon, 1985) p. 238.
2. Louis Raths, Merrill Harmin, and Sidney Simon, *Values and Teaching: Working with Values in the Classroom* (Columbus, Ohio: Charles E. Merrill Publishing Co., 1966), p. 28.
3. Dean Turner, *Commitment to Care* (Devin Adair Publishing Co.) Used by permission.
4. Dwight Boyd and Deanne Bogden, "Something Clarified, Nothing of Value," *Educational Theory 3,* Vol. 34 (Summer 1984), p. 292.
5. Dean Turner, *Commitment to Care* (Devin Adair Publishing Co.).
6. Louis Raths, Merrill Harmin, and Sidney Simon, *Values and Teaching: Working with Values in the Classroom* (Columbus, Ohio: Charles E. Merrill Publishing Co., 1966), pp. 38-39.
7. Kathleen Gow, *Yes, Virginia, There Is Right and Wrong* (Wheaton, Illinois: Tyndale House Pub., Inc., 1985), p. 30. Quoted from Louis Raths, Merrill Harmin, and Sidney Simon, *Values and Teaching: Working with*

Values in the Classroom, 2nd Ed. (Columbus, Ohio: Charles E. Merrill Publishing Co.), p. 48.

8. *Ibid.*, 1st Edition, p. 227.

9. Clifford E. Knapp, "The Value of Values Clarification: A Reaction to the Critics," *The Journal of Environmental Education 2*, Vol. 13 (Winter 1981-82), p. 2.

10. Raths, et al., 1st Ed., pp. 39-40.

11. Alan T. Lockwood, "A Critical View of Values Clarification," *The Elementary School Journal 1*, Vol. 77, Columbia University (Sept., 1975), pp. 35-50.

12. Martin Eger, "The Conflict in Moral Education: An Informal Case Study," *Education: Annual Editions 1983-84*, Fred Shultz, Ed. (Sluice Dock, Guilford, Conn: The Dushkin Publishing Group, Inc., 1983-84), pp. 98-106.

13. Maury Smith, *A Practical Guide to Values Clarification* (San Diego: University Associates, 1977), pp. 120-121. This was first brought to our attention in Gow's *Yes, Virginia, There Is Right and Wrong*, pp. 35-38.

14. Wendell R. Bird, "Freedom of Religion and Science Instruction in the Public Schools," *The Yale Law Journal 3*, Vol. 87 (January 1978), p. 523.

15. Congressman John B. Conlan, "The MACOS Controversy," *Social Education* (October, 1975), pp. 29, 390.

16. H.C. Hudgins, Jr. and Richard Vacca, *Law and Education: Contemporary Issues and Court Decisions* (Charlottesville, Virginia: The Michie Company, 1979), p. 172. Court case referred to is *Valent v. New Jersey State Board of Education*, 274 A.2d 832 (N.J. 1971).

Chapter 5

1. Joseph F. Lagana, *What Happens to the Attitudes of Beginning Teachers* (Danville, Illinois: The Interstate Printers and Publishers, Inc., 1971), p. 5. Also see Kevin Ryan, *Don't Smile Until Christmas* (Chicago: University of Chicago Press, 1970), p. 175.

2. Hans N. Sheridan, *Clarification of Management Rights to Student Due Process in Indiana* (accredited dissertation), (1701 Pemberton Dr., Ft. Wayne, Indiana, copyright 1980), p. 21. Sheridan's remark is grounded in *Goss v. Lopez*, 419 U.S. 739 (1975).

3. *Ibid* p. 69. See also E. Edmund Reutter, Jr., *The Courts and Student Conduct* (Topeka, Kansas: National Organization on Legal Problems of Education, 1975).

4. Sheridan, p. 13. *Goss v. Lopez,* 419 U.S. 565 (1975).
5. *Goss v. Lopez,* 419 U.S. 565, 95 S. Ct. 729, 42 L. Ed. 2d 725 (1975). First brought to our attention in H.C. Hudgins, Jr. and Richard S. Vacca, *Law and Education: Contemporary Issues and Court Decisions* (Charlottesville, Virginia: The Michie Co., 1979), p. 238.
6. *Baker v. Owens,* 395 F Supp. 294 (M.D.N.C. 1975), aff'd mem, 423 U.S. 907, and *Ingraham v. Wright,* 430 U.S. 657, 97 S. Ct. 1401, 51 L. Ed. 2d 711 (1977).
7. *Frank v. Orleans Parish School Bd.,* 195 So. 2d 451 (La. 1967).
8. *Landi v. West Chester Area School District,* 353 A 2d 895 (Pa. 1976).
9. *People v. Ball,* 58 Ill. 2d 96, 317 N.E. 2d 54 (1974).
10. *Tinkham v. Kole,* 110 N.W. 2d 258 (Iowa 1961), and *Caffas v. Board of School Directors,* 353 A 2d 898 (Pa. 1976).
11. *Ladson v. Board of Education,* 323 N.Y.S. 2d 545 (N.Y. 1971).
12. *Knight v. Board of Education,* 38 Ill., App. 3d 603, 348 N.E. 2d 299 (1976), and *Dorsey v. Bale,* 521 S.W. 2d 76 (C.A. Ky., 1975).
13. Quotation from Hudgins, Jr. and Vacca, p. 248. *People v. V.D.,* 34 N.Y. 2d 483, 315 N.E. 2d 466 (1974).
14. Hudgins, Jr. and Vacca, p. 248. Italics in quotation ours. *Bellnier v. Lund,* 438 F. Supp., 47 (N.D. N.Y. 1977).
15. *Jacobs v. Board of School Commissioners of City of Indianapolis,* 490 F. 2nd 60 (Seventh Circuit 1973).
16. *Tinker v. Des Moines,* 393 U.S. 506 (1969). Italics ours. This was first brought to our attention by Hans N. Sheridan (see ref. No. 2).

Chapter 6

1. *Violent Schools—Safe Schools: The Safe School Study Report to the Congress* (U.S. Department of Health, Education, and Welfare; National Institute of Education, January, 1978), p. iii, and Appendix B-4.
2. *Ibid,* p. iii.
3. *Ibid,* p. iii.
4. *Ibid,* Appendix B-4.

Chapter 8

1. *Social Education* (April, 1982), Volume 46, No. 4, pp. 274-275.

TABLE OF CASES

Jaffree, Wallace et. al. v., 472 U.S. ___, 105 S.Ct. ___, 86 L.Ed.2d 29 (1985)
James v. Board of Education, 461 F.2d 566 (2 Cir. 1972)

Keefe v. Geanakos, 418 F.2d 359 (1 Cir. 1969)
Knight v. Board of Education, 348 N.E.2d 299 (1976)
Kole, Tinkham v., 110 N.W.2d 258 (Iowa 1961)
Kurtzman, Lemon v., 403 U.S. 602, 91 S.Ct. 2105, 29 L.Ed.2d 745 (1971)

Ladson v. Board of Education, 323 N.Y.S.2d 545 (N.Y. 1971)
LaFleur, Cleveland Board of Education v., 414 U.S. 632, 94 S.Ct. 791, 39 L.Ed.2d 52 (1974)
LaMont v. Postmaster General, 381 U.S. 301, 85 S.Ct. 1493, 14 L.Ed.2d 398 (1956)
Landi v. West Chester Area School District, 353 A.2d 895 (Pa. 1976)
Lemon v. Kurtzman, 403 U.S. 602, 91 S.Ct. 2105, 29 L.Ed.2d 745 (1971)
Lopez, Goss v., 419 U.S. 565, 95 S.Ct. 729, 42 L.Ed. 725 (1975)
Lund, Bellnier v., 438 F.Supp. 47 (N.D. N.Y. 1977)

Maharishi Mahesh Yogi, Malnak v., 440 F.Supp. 1284 (1977), affirmed 592 F.2d 197 (1979)
Malnak v. Maharishi Mahesh Yogi, 440 F.Supp. 1284 (1977), affirmed 592 F.2d 197 (1979)
McCollum v. Board of Education, Illinois ex rel, 303 U.S. 203, 68 S.Ct. 461, 92 L.Ed. 649 (1948)
Meyer v. Nebraska, 262 U.S. 390, 43 S.Ct. 625, 67 L.Ed. 1042 (1923)

Nebraska, Meyer v., 262 U.S. 390, 43 S.Ct. 625, 67 L.Ed. 1042 (1923)

Orleans Parish School Board, Frank v., 195 So.2d 451 (La. 1967)
Owens, Baker v., 395 F.Supp. 294 (M.D.N.C. 1975), affirmed 423 U.S. 907

Page, Davis v., 385 F.Supp. 395 (1974)
Panarella v. Birenbaum, 343 N.Y.S.2d 333 (1973)
People v. V.D., 315 N.E.2d 466 (1974)
Pico, Island Trees Union Free School District v., 50 U.S.L.W. 4831 (1982)

Review Board of Indiana, Thomas v., 450 U.S. 707, 101 S.Ct. 1425, 67 L.Ed.2d 624 (1981)
Rodriguez, San Antonio School Board v., 411 U.S. 1, 93 S.Ct. 1278, 36 L.Ed.2d 16 (1973)
Roe v. Wade, 410 U.S. 113, 93 S.Ct. 705, 35 L.Ed.2d 147 (1973)

San Antonio School Board v. Rodriguez, 411 U.S. 1, 93 S.Ct. 1278, 36 L.Ed.2d 16 (1973)

Schempp, Abington Township v., 374 U.S. 203, 83 S.Ct. 1560, 10 L.Ed.2d
    844 (1963)
Seeger, U.S. v., 380 U.S. 163, 85 S.Ct. 850, 13 L.Ed.2d 733 (1965)
Segraves v. California (No. 278978, Dept. 15, California 1981)
Smithsonian Institution, Crowley v., 636 F.2d 738 (D.C. Cir. 1980)
Stanley v. Illinois, 405 U.S. 645, 92 S.Ct. 1208, 31 L.Ed.2d 551 (1972)

Tinker v. Des Moines Independent Community School District, 393 U.S.
    503, 80 S.Ct. 733, 21 L.Ed. 731 (1969)
Tinkham v. Kole, 110 N.W.2d 258 (Iowa 1961)
Thomas v. Review Board of Indiana, 450 U.S. 707, 101 S.Ct. 1425, 67 L.Ed.2d
    624 (1981)
Torcaso v. Watkins, 367 U.S. 488, 81 S.Ct. 1680, 6 L.Ed.2d 982 (1961)

United States v. Seeger, 380 U.S. 163, 85 S.Ct. 850, 13 L.Ed.2d 733 (1965)

V.D., People v., 315 N.E.2d 466 (1974)
Valent v. New Jersey State Board of Education, 274 A.2d 832 (1971)
Vincent v. Widmar, 454 U.S. 263, 102 S.Ct. 269 (1981)
Vitale, Engel v., 370 U.S. 97, 82 S.Ct. 1261, 8 L.Ed.2d 601 (1962)

Wade, Roe v., 410 U.S. 113, 93 S.Ct. 705, 35 L.Ed.2d 147 (1973)
Wallace, et. al., v. Jaffree, 472 U.S. _____, 105 S.Ct. _____, 86 L.Ed.2d 29 (1985)
Watkins, Torcaso v., 367 U.S. 488, 81 S.Ct. 1680, 6 L.Ed.2d 982 (1961)
West Chester Area School District, Landi v., 353 A.2d 895 (Pa. 1976)
Widmar v. Vincent, 454 U.S. 263, 102 S.Ct. (1981)
Williamsport v. Bender, pending in U.S. Supreme Court as of February 11,
    1986
Wisconsin v. Yoder, 406 U.S. 205, 92 S.Ct. 1526, 32 L.Ed.2d 15 (1972)
Wright, Ingraham v., 430 U.S. 657, 97 S.Ct. 1401, 51 L.Ed.2d 711 (1977)

Yoder, Wisconsin v., 406 U.S. 205, 92 S.Ct. 1526, 32 L.Ed.2d 15 (1972)

Zorach v. Clauson, 343 U.S. 306, 72 S.Ct. 679, 96 L.Ed. 954 (1952)

Appendix A

The Hatch Amendment and Accompanying U.S. Department of Education Regulations

Protection of Pupil Rights
20 U.S. Code §1232h

Inspection by parents or guardians of instructional material.

(a) All instructional material, including teacher's manuals, films, tapes, or other supplementary instructional material which will be used in connection with any research or experimentation program or project shall be available for inspection by the parents or guardians of the children engaged in such program or project. For the purpose of this section "research or experimentation program or project" means any program or project in any applicable program designed to explore or develop new or unproven teaching methods or techniques.

Psychiatric or psychological
examinations, testing, or treatment.

(b) No student shall be required, as part of any applicable program, to submit to psychiatric examination, testing, or treatment, or psychological examination, testing, or treatment, in which the primary purpose is to reveal information concerning:

(1) political affiliations;

(2) mental and psychological problems potentially embarrassing to the student or his family;

(3) sex behavior and attitudes;

(4) illegal, anti-social, self-incriminating and demeaning behavior;

(5) critical appraisals of other individuals with whom respondents have close family relationships;

(6) legally recognized privileged and analogous relationships, such as those of lawyers, physicians, and ministers; or

(7) income (other than that required by law to determine eligibility for participation in a program or for receiving financial assistance under such program),

without the prior consent of the student (if the student is an adult or

188

emancipated minor), or in the case of unemancipated minor, without the prior written consent of the parent.

34 CFR Part 98—Student Rights in Research, Experimental Programs, and Testing

§98.1 Applicability of part.

This part applies to any program administered by the Secretary of Education that—

(a)(1) Was transferred to the Department by the Department of Education Organization Act (DEOA); and

(2) Was administered by the Education Division of the Department of Health, Education, and Welfare on the day before the effective date of the DEOA; or

(b) Was enacted after the effective date of the DEOA, unless the law enacting the new Federal program has the effect of making section 439 of the General Education Provisions Act inapplicable.

* * *

§98.3 Access to Instructional material used in a research or experimentation program.

(a) All instructional material—including teachers' manuals, films, tapes, or other supplementary instructional material—which will be used in connection with any research or experimentation program or project shall be available for inspection by the parents or guardians of the children engaged in such program or project.

(b) For the purpose of this part "research or experimentation program or project" means any program or project in any program under §98.1 (a) or (b) that is designed to explore or develop new or unproven teaching methods or techniques.

(c) For the purpose of the section "children" means persons not above age 21 who are enrolled in a program under §98.1 (a) or (b) not above the elementary or secondary education level, as determined under State law.

§98.4 Protection of students' privacy in examination, testing, or treatment.

(a) No student shall be required, as part of any program specified in §98.1 (a) or (b), to submit without prior consent to psychiatric examination, testing, or treatment, or psychological examination, testing, or treatment, in which the primary purpose is to reveal information

concerning one or more of the following—
(1) Political affiliations;
(2) Mental and psychological problems potentially embarrassing to the student or his or her family;
(3) Sex behavior and attitudes;
(4) Illegal, anti-social, self-incriminating and demeaning behavior;
(5) Critical appraisals of other individuals with whom the student has close family relationships;
(6) Legally recognized privileged and analogous relationships, such as those of lawyers, physicians, and ministers; or
(7) Income, other than that required by law to determine eligibility for participation in a program or for receiving financial assistance under a program.
(b) As used in paragraph (a) of this section, "prior consent" means—
(1) Prior consent of the student, if the student is an adult or emancipated minor; or
(2) Prior written consent of the parent or guardian, if the student is an unemancipated minor.
(c) As used in paragraph (a) of this section—
(1) "Psychiatric or psychological examination or test" means a method of obtaining information, including a group activity, that is not directly related to academic instruction and that is designed to elicit information about attitudes, habits, traits, opinions, beliefs or feelings; and
(2) "Psychiatric or psychological treatment" means an activity involving the planned, systematic use of methods or techniques that are not directly related to academic instruction and that is designed to affect behavioral, emotional, or attitudinal characteristics of an individual or group.

§98.5 Information and Investigation office.
(a) The Secretary has designated an office to provide information about the requirements of section 439 of the Act, and to investigate, process, and review complaints that may be filed concerning alleged violations of the provisions of the section.
(b) The following is the name and address of the office designated under paragraph (a) of this section: Family Educational Rights and Privacy Act Office, U.S. Department of Education, 400 Maryland Avenue, SW., Washington, D.C. 20202.

§98.6 Reports.
The Secretary may require the recipient to submit reports containing

information necessary to resolve complaints under Section 439 of the Act and the regulations in this part.

§98.7 Filing a complaint.

(a) Only a student or a parent or guardian of a student directly affected by a violation under Section 439 of the Act may file a complaint under this part. The complaint must be submitted in writing to the Office.

(b) The complaint filed under paragraph (a) of this section must—

(1) Contain specific allegations of fact giving reasonable cause to believe that a violation of either §98.3 or §98.4 exists; and

(2) Include evidence of attempted resolution of the complaint at the local level (and at the State level if a State complaint resolution process exists), including the names of local and State officials contacted and significant dates in the attempted resolution process.

(c) The Office investigates each complaint which the Office receives that meets the requirements of this section to determine whether the recipient or contractor failed to comply with the provisions of Section 439 of the Act.

§98.8 Notice of the complaint.

(a) If the Office receives a complaint that meets the requirements of §98.7, it provides written notification to the complainant and the recipient or contractor against which the violation has been alleged that the complaint has been received.

(b) The notice to the recipient or contractor under paragraph (a) of this section must—

(1) Include the substance of the alleged violation; and

(2) Inform the recipient or contractor that the Office will investigate the complaint and that the recipient or contractor may submit a written response to the complaint.

§98.9 Investigation and findings.

(a) The Office may permit the parties to submit further written or oral arguments or information.

(b) Following its investigations, the Office provides to the complainant and recipient or contractor written notice of its findings and the basis for its findings.

(c) If the Office finds that the recipient or contractor has not complied with Section 439 of the Act, the Office includes in its notice under paragraph (b) of this section—

(1) A statement of the specific steps that the Secretary recommends the

191

recipient or contractor take to comply; and

(2) Provides a reasonable period of time, given all of the circumstances of the case, during which the recipient or contractor may comply voluntarily.

§98.10 Enforcement of the findings.

(a) If the recipient or contractor does not comply during the period of time set under §98.9(c), the Secretary may either—

(1) For a recipient, take an action authorized under 34 CFR Part 78, including—

(i) Issuing a notice of intent to terminate funds under 34 CFR 78.21;

(ii) Issuing a notice to withhold funds under 34 CFR 78.21, 200.94(b), or 298.45(b), depending upon the applicable program under which the notice is issued; or

(iii) Issuing a notice to cease and desist under 34 CFR 78.31, 200.94(c) or 298.45(c), depending upon the program under which the notice is issued; or

(2) For a contractor, direct the contracting officer to take an appropriate action authorized under the Federal Acquisition Regulations, including either—

(i) Issuing a notice to suspend operations under 48 CFR 12.5; or

(ii) Issuing a notice to terminate for default, either in whole or in part under 48 CFR 49.102.

(b) If, after an investigation under §98.9, the Secretary finds that a recipient or contractor has complied voluntarily with Section 439 of the Act, the Secretary provides the complainant and the recipient or contractor written notice of the decision and the basis for the decision.

Federal Register, vol. 49, no. 174, Sept. 6, 1984, pp. 35321-35222.

Appendix B

The "Hatch Letter"

Date: _____

To: School Board President _____

Dear _____:

I am the parent of _____ who attends _____ _____ School. Under U.S. legislation and court decisions, parents have the primary responsibility for their children's education, and pupils have certain rights which the schools may not deny. Parents have the right to assure that their children's beliefs and moral values are not undermined by the schools. Pupils have the right to have and to hold their values and moral standards without direct or indirect manipulation by the schools through curricula, textbooks, audio-visual materials, or supplementary assignments.

Accordingly, I hereby request that my child be involved in NO school activities or materials listed below unless I have first reviewed all the relevant materials and have given my written consent for their use:

Psychological and psychiatric examinations, tests, or surveys that are designed to elicit information about attitudes, habits, traits, opinions, beliefs, or feelings of an individual or group;

Psychological and psychiatric treatment that is designed to affect behavior, emotional, or attitudinal characteristics of an individual or group;

Values clarification, use of moral dilemmas, discussion of religious or moral standards, role-playing or open-ended discussions of situations involving moral issues, and survival games including life/death decision exercises;

Death education, including abortion, euthanasia, suicide, use of violence, and discussion of death and dying;

Curricula pertaining to alcohol and drugs;

Instruction in nuclear war, nuclear policy, and nuclear classroom games;

Anti-nationalistic, one-world government or globalism curricula;

Discussion and testing on inter-personal relationships; discussions of attitudes toward parents and parenting;

Education in human sexuality, including premarital sex, extra-marital sex, contraception, abortion, homosexuality, group sex and marriages, prostitution, incest, masturbation, bestiality, divorce, population control, and roles of males and females; sex behavior and attitudes of student and family;

Pornography and any materials containing profanity and/or sexual explicitness;

Guided fantasy techniques; hypnotic techniques; imagery and suggestology;

Organic evolution, including the idea that man has developed from previous or lower types of living things;

Discussions of witchcraft, occultism, the supernatural, and Eastern mysticism;

Political affiliations and beliefs of student and family; personal religious beliefs and practices;

Mental and psychological problems and self-incriminating behavior potentially embarrassing to the student or family;

Critical appraisals of other individuals with whom the child has family relationships;

Legally recognized privileged and analogous relationships, such as those of lawyers, physicians, and ministers;

Income, including the student's role in family activities and finances;

Non-academic personality tests; questionnaires on personal and family life and attitudes;

Autobiography assignments; log books, diaries, and personal journals;

Contrived incidents for self-revelation; sensitivity training, group encounter sessions, talk-ins, magic circle techniques, self-evaluation and auto-criticism; strategies designed for self-disclosure (e.g., zig-zag);

Sociograms; sociodrama; psychodrama; blindfold walks; isolation techniques.

The purpose of this letter is to preserve my child's rights under the Protection of Pupil Rights Amendment (the Hatch Amendment) to the General Education Provisions Act, and under its regulations as published in the *Federal Register* of Sept. 6, 1984, which became effective Nov. 12, 1984. These regulations provide a procedure for filing complaints first at the local level, and then with the U.S. Department of Education. If a voluntary remedy fails, federal funds can be withdrawn from those in violation of the law. I respectfully ask you to send me a substantive response to this letter attaching a copy of your policy statement on procedures for parental permission requirements, to notify all my child's teachers, and to keep a copy of this letter in my child's permanent file. Thank you for your cooperation.

Sincerely, _____

copy to School Principal

Appendix C

Colorado Springs Public Schools
School District Number Eleven

ADMINISTRATIVE PROCEDURES FOR SELECTION OF
MEDIA IN UNIQUE COLLECTIONS
(Such as school library media centers, Professional
Resource Center, Special Education Resource Center, etc.)

A. Definition

Media included in unique collections are those materials for which primary selection is made by individual(s) rather than a committee. All media purchased through the district, building and/or private funds, gifts, free and/or borrowed materials must be selected through this procedure.

B. Introduction

This procedure recognizes that it is the privilege, right, and responsibility of professional educators to select media suitable to the abilities and needs of students in relation to both the curriculum and to personal interests of students and their teachers. This procedure further recognizes that it is the privilege, right, and responsibility of the public (educators, students and community citizens) to question any media that they may consider to be inappropriate.

This procedure further recognizes the right of parents to request that their child may be given alternative materials or assignments.

This procedure recognizes the right of any parent to determine what materials may be used with their child.

195

This procedure recognizes any judgment a teacher and/or media specialist makes in the utilization of materials which are not selected within this process are the sole responsibility of that teacher and/or media specialist.

C. Responsibility
1. Legal
    The Board of Education of the Colorado Springs Public School District Eleven is legally responsible for school media which is prescribed in the district instructional program.
2. Supervision
    The Board of Education delegates the responsibility for selection to the administrative staff. The responsibility for coordinating and/or supervising the selection rests with the appropriate administrative assistant and/or supervisor.
3. Implementation
    The administrative staff delegates the final selection to the certified professional media specialist, supervisor, and/or elementary principal. Regardless of funding, the responsibility for purchase lies with the certified media specialist for that school, special collections supervisor, and/or with the building principal.

D. Assumptions
1. A collection should be balanced to reflect the many elements present in the curriculum and society.
2. A collection should be balanced in relation to a specific topic to represent various viewpoints of an issue.
3. A collection should reflect the student's right to study a controversial issue which has political, economic, or social significance.
4. A collection should reflect the pluralistic character and culture of our society.
5. A collection should reflect an attitude of fostering respect for minority groups, women, religious and social differences and ethnic groups.
6. The physical format of any media item shall not be altered in any way.
7. Any citizen who lives within the boundaries of School District Eleven or any employee of School District Eleven shall have the right to participate in the selection and retention of all media used within any school.

8. Citizen participation is designed to reinforce and augment the professional judgments of individual media specialists and teachers in the selection and use of media.
9. Media should be selected for their major strengths.
10. A collection should reflect and recognize student differences.

E. Criteria for Selection of Media
The following selection criteria may be used as they apply.
1. General. Materials chosen should/may:
   a. Meet the needs and goals of an individual school collection
   b. Contain appealing content and style to suit the interests and abilities of students
   c. Have a suitable physical format and appearance
   d. Meet the needs of the exceptional as well as the average student
   e. Reflect a valid and reliable viewpoint on the part of the author
   f. Be appropriate for the maturity and ability of the students
   g. Contain biased or slanted viewpoints only to meet specific curricular needs
   h. Stimulate creativity
2. Fiction. Materials chosen should/may:
   a. Have literary value
   b. Portray intergroup tension and conflict objectivity
   c. Reflect societal problems, aspirations, attitudes and ideals
   d. Represent literary quality to include appropriate setting, point of view, characters, plot, theme and style
3. Nonfiction. Materials chosen should/may:
   a. Cover a subject of importance and interest
   b. Reflect knowledge or research on the part of the author
   c. Be up-to-date where appropriate
   d. Meet high standards of quality in factual content
   e. Be appropriate for the subject area and grade level
   f. Meet high standards in format (e.g., maps, illustrations, type face, bibliographies, indices)
   g. Be organized in a logical sequence
   h. Not manipulate facts to further a specific point of view

F. Procedures for Selection of Media
1. In selecting materials for purchase for the media center, the

media specialist, elementary principal, and/or special collections supervisor shall evaluate the existing collection and the curricular needs and will consult reputable, professionally prepared selection aids, professional journals and other appropriate sources. For the purpose of this procedure the term "media" includes all materials considered part of the library media collection, plus all instructional materials housed in resource centers and classroom (if any) which are not text materials. For the purpose of this procedure, the term "media center" is the space, room or complex of rooms and spaces designated as a library media center, resource center or similar term. It may include units not contiguous to the center where facilities dictate. These units will include but not be limited to resource centers, production centers, and television studios.

2. In selecting materials for purchase for the media center, the media specialist, elementary principal and/or special collections supervisor will seek input from staff and students. Input may be in the form of recommendations for purchase, techniques for utilization and suggestions for improvement of the media program. Input may be formal and/or informal.

3. Gift materials shall be judged by the criteria listed in Section E and shall be accepted or rejected by those criteria.

4. Selection is an ongoing process which shall include the removal of media (weeding) because of:
   a. Deteriorated physical condition
   b. Multiplicity of copies
   c. Out-of-date or obsolete information
   d. Lack of circulation over an extended length of time
   e. Failure to meet current selection criteria or selection process

5. Selection and approval of media requests are the responsibilities of the principal and the media specialist, when available for that school; and/or special collections supervisor.

6. Approved media requests are submitted to the appropriate administrative assistant and delegated to the media supervisor and/or special collections supervisor for review privileges, including challenge or rejection.

7. In cases where requests for media items are challenged and/or rejected by the media supervisor and/or special collections supervisor, a notation of the media title with reasons for its rejection should be furnished to the principal, building media

specialist or teacher and to the Assistant Superintendent for Instructional Services. If the selection cannot be resolved at this level it will be referred to a representative standing review committee called Media Review Committee comprised of two building media specialists, two principals, two teachers and two Instructional Services personnel. Elementary and secondary levels will be equally represented on the committee.

The committee will be appointed by the Assistant Superintendent for Instructional Services after consulting with the appropriate professional associations. This committee will serve for one school year. The committee may be called into session at the request of either party involved in the challenge.

The committee will consider and act on the challenge. A written copy of the committee's decision will be provided to the appropriate supervisor, building principal, building media specialist and the Assistant Superintendent for Instructional Services within fifteen (15) days.

In the event of appeal from a decision made at the second level, the Board of Education will have all information on the activities and decisions which have occurred prior to this time. The Board of Education will then review preceding decisions before announcing its decision.

G. Procedures for Reconsideration of Media Located in Unique Collections

Step A Concerns about learning resources, written or verbal, shall be directed to the school principal, who will officially acknowledge them within five (5) school days. In the event the principal is the person expressing concern, an unbiased person shall be appointed by the Assistant Superintendent for Instructional Services to conduct the procedure. In the event the principal is unavailable, the assistant or acting principal shall begin the procedure.

Step B The principal or designee shall attempt to resolve the issue of the concern informally by explaining the rationale for selection and use of the item as defined in this procedure to the person expressing the concern within five (5) school days after the scheduled meeting with the person expressing concern. Removal of the item is not an option at this step.

Step C If the person expressing a concern is not satisfied to have the item remain in use, the principal shall ask that a signed "Statement of Concern About Learning Resources" form be completed. All formal concerns must be made on this form. Media under question can be withdrawn only by action of a building committee, district committee or Board of Education. (Under unusual and extreme conditions, the principal may temporarily withdraw media not to exceed the length of time of the committee hearing(s).

Step D Upon receipt of the completed form, the principal requests that the review of the media by the building committee be completed within fifteen (15) school days. The principal notifies the person expressing concern, the Assistant Superintendent for Instructional Services and Supervisor, Media Services in writing that such a review is being done. Notification shall include a copy of the completed form, composition of the committee and the date of the meeting. In accordance with Colorado's Open Meetings Law (C.R.S. 24-6-401 and 402), any number of observers may be present.

    1. The composition of the odd numbered elementary and secondary committees will be as follows:

        a. (1) Principal or designee (chairperson)

            (2) Three to five (3-5) teachers from building

            (3) Colorado certified media specialist from LRS or secondary school

            (4) One to three (1-3) citizens from school community

            (5) Ex-officio Members (nonvoting):

                (a) Resource Center Technician

                (b) Interested teachers from building

                (c) Instructional Services representative

                (d) Not more than two (2) individuals or organizational representatives requesting the reconsideration

                (e) Recorder of minutes

        b. Secondary

            (1) Principal or designee (chairperson)

     (2) Certified media specialist from LRS or another secondary school

     (3) Three to five (3-5) teachers from building

     (4) One to three (1-3) citizens from school community

     (5) One (1) student representative may be included at the discretion of the principal

     (6) Ex-officio Members (nonvoting):
- (a) Media Specialist
- (b) Interested teachers from building
- (c) Instructional Services representative
- (d) Not more than two (2) individuals or organizational representatives requesting the reconsideration
- (e) Recorder of minutes

2. The principal shall provide each committee member (not ex-officio) with the following:
   a. Copy of item
   b. Copy of completed forms
   c. Copy(s) of reviews from professional journals as provided by the media specialist and/or supervisor
   d. Copy of Selection Policy

3. Each committee member shall:
   a. Review Introduction statement of these procedures
   b. Review item in entirety
   c. Complete "Committee Review of Media" form at committee meeting

4. The principal shall conduct the committee meeting to include the following:
   a. Define the concern
   b. Review the Introduction statement
   c. Determine whether the item meets selection criteria
   d. Direct the discussion by official and ex-officio members of the committee
   e. Call for the completion of "Committee Review of Media" forms
   f. Bring closure with written vote on "Committee Review of Media" form

201

5. The principal shall provide a written copy of the committee's decision to the person expressing concern within ten (10) school days after the date of the building committee meeting with a timetable and explanation of the appeal process.

6. The principal shall provide a written copy of the committee's decision, minutes of the meeting and the "Committee Review of Media" forms to the Assistant Superintendent for Instructional Services.

7. When the simple majority vote of the building committee results in removal of the item, the principal will send all copies of said item to Learning Resource Services (LRS) after removing them from appropriate inventory records.

Step E   The Assistant Superintendent for Instructional Services shall provide the appropriate supervisor, the superintendent and/or school board with appropriate information regarding any actions taken as the result of the request for reconsideration of media within the building within ten (10) school days.

Step F   The person expressing concern has the right to appeal the decision of the building committee within fifteen (15) school days from the date of building committee hearing. This written request should be directed to the Assistant Superintendent for Instructional Services.

1. Upon the receipt of the appeal request, the Assistant Superintendent for Instructional Services shall form an odd-numbered committee to reconsider the concern about the media item within fifteen (15) school days from the date this request was received. No voting member of the building committee may serve as a voting member of this committee.

2. The composition of the odd-numbered committee shall be as follows:

   a. Assistant Superintendent for Instructional Services or designee
   b. Three to five (3-5) instructional supervisors
   c. One (1) media supervisor or certified media specialist
   d. One to three (1-3) citizens of the district community

e. Ex-officio Members (nonvoting):
   (1) Person(s) expressing concern
   (2) Principal or designee
   (3) Recorder of minutes

3. The Assistant Superintendent for Instructional Services and committee members shall follow the same procedures as used at the building committee. (See Step D.2, D.3, D.4)

4. The Assistant Superintendent shall provide a written copy of the committee's decision, minutes of the meeting and the "Committee Review of Media" forms for the archival records housed at Learning Resources Services (LRS).

5. When the simple majority vote of the district committee results in removal of the item, the principal will send all copies of said item to Learning Resource Services (LRS) after removing them from appropriate inventory records.

6. The Assistant Superintendent for Instructional Services shall provide the person expressing concern, building principal, the superintendent and/or school board with appropriate information regarding any actions taken as a result of the request for reconsideration of media within ten (10) school days.

Step G   The person expressing concern has the right to appeal the decision of the district committee within fifteen (15) school days of the date of the committee report. This written request should be sent to the Superintendent.

1. The Superintendent shall acknowledge the receipt of the request for appeal within fifteen (15) school days and will provide the person expressing concern with appropriate information concerning the Superintendent or Board of Education review of the questioned media item.

Step H   An item which has undergone reconsideration may not be reconsidered in that building for ninety (90) school days from the date of the report of the building committee.

Step I   In the event of a severe overload of concerns, the principal, after completing Step C, may elect to postpone Step D for a reasonable time agreed upon by both parties.

Step J   An item may be removed from a building only as a result of a concern initiated in that specific building or by a decision of the Board of Education as a result of a concern appealed to the Superintendent/Board of Education.

Step K   When a media item is removed from a collection at any level, it shall be reviewed upon request in twenty-four (24) months by the Media Review Committee (as defined in Section E, number 7). The Media Review Committee may recommend by a simple majority vote to reenter said item into the appropriate collection or may recommend by a simple majority vote to sustain the removal for an additional twelve (12) school months. The person(s) expressing concern, principal and appropriate supervisor shall be notified of the review meeting with attendance optional. Responsibility for scheduling and coordinating this process shall rest with the Supervisor, Media Services.

Appendix D
End of Year Survey to Parents and Teachers

Source: Cherry Creek School District No. 5, Englewood, Colorado, A. Thel Kocher, Director, Research and Evaluation.

(SA — STRONGLY AGREE; A — AGREE; DA — DISAGREE; SD — STRONGLY DISAGREE)

1. Please circle one response to indicate how much you agree with each of the following statements.

Teachers use appropriate instructional methods.	SA	A	DA	SD
Teachers use appropriate methods to assess student progress.	SA	A	DA	SD
Teachers appropriately manage their daily program.	SA	A	DA	SD
Teachers initiate contact with parents when necessary and desirable.	SA	A	DA	SD
I feel free to contact the teachers when necessary.	SA	A	DA	SD

(SA = STRONGLY AGREE; A = AGREE; DA = DISAGREE; SD = STRONGLY DISAGREE)

The principal provides strong professional leadership.	SA	A	DA	SD
I feel free to contact the principal when necessary.	SA	A	DA	SD
The school environment encourages learning.	SA	A	DA	SD
Children behave appropriately in the lunchroom.	SA	A	DA	SD
Computers are used effectively.	SA	A	DA	SD
The curriculum is satisfactorily explained to parents.	SA	A	DA	SD
The school policies are appropriately enforced.	SA	A	DA	SD
The amount of school time students spend on academics is sufficient.	SA	A	DA	SD
_____ adequately provides for the needs of gifted/talented students.	SA	A	DA	SD
_____ adequately provides for the needs of students having academic difficulty.	SA	A	DA	SD
_____ adequately provides for the needs of students who have a "handicapping" condition.	SA	A	DA	SD
When students complete the program at _____ they will be adequately prepared for the next level of education.	SA	A	DA	SD
The office staff is courteous and helpful.	SA	A	DA	SD
The nurse is helpful.	SA	A	DA	SD
Discipline is fair.	SA	A	DA	SD
Discipline should be more firm.	SA	A	DA	SD
Discipline should be less firm.	SA	A	DA	SD

(SA = STRONGLY AGREE; A = AGREE; DA = DISAGREE; SD = STRONGLY DISAGREE)

Parent-teacher conferences are useful.	SA	A	DA	SD
I feel welcome when I visit _____.	SA	A	DA	SD
_____ has an appropriate way for accepting parent input into planning.	SA	A	DA	SD

2. Overall, how do you rate the *quality* of each of the following at _____ _____? (Circle one response for each.)

(HQ = HIGH QUALITY; OK = OKAY; LQ = LOW QUALITY)

Reading	HQ	OK	LQ	Instrumental Music	HQ	OK	LQ
Mathematics	HQ	OK	LQ				
Writing (Composition)	HQ	OK	LQ	Art	HQ	OK	LQ
				Physical Education	HQ	OK	LQ
Handwriting	HQ	OK	LQ				
Spelling	HQ	OK	LQ	Extracurricular Activities	HQ	OK	LQ
Grammar	HQ	OK	LQ	Media Education	HQ	OK	LQ
Social Studies	HQ	OK	LQ				
General Science	HQ	OK	LQ	Efforts to provide a positive learning environment for each student	HQ	OK	LQ
Health Education	HQ	OK	LQ				
General Music	HQ	OK	LQ				

3. Overall, what "grade" would you give each of the following? (Circle one response for each.)

The Educational Program at _____.	A B C D Fail
The Teachers at _____.	A B C D Fail
The Principal at _____.	A B C D Fail
The _____ facility.	A B C D Fail

4. Please indicate the grade level of the *eldest* child you have at this school.

> K   1   2   3   4   5   6

Just how much does this child enjoy going to school?

> Very Much   Somewhat   Very Little

5. With regard to this *eldest* child, please circle one response to indicate how much you agree with each of the following statements.

Teacher's plan instruction to meet my child's needs.	SA	A	DA	SD
I understand the written progress reports I receive.	SA	A	DA	SD
The written progress reports provide the information I need.	SA	A	DA	SD
My child's work is too difficult.	SA	A	DA	SD
My child's work is too easy.	SA	A	DA	SD
My child receives too much homework.	SA	A	DA	SD
My child does not receive enough homework.	SA	A	DA	SD
_____ provides adequate support for my child's social/emotional needs.	SA	A	DA	SD
_____ keeps me well informed about my child's progress.	SA	A	DA	SD

6. About how much time per week does the *eldest* child spend

Watching TV?	0 hrs.	1-5 hrs.	6-10 hrs.	11-15 hrs.	15+ hrs.
Doing homework?	0 hrs.	1-5 hrs.	6-10 hrs.	11-15 hrs.	15+ hrs.

About how much time per week do you as (a) parent(s) spend helping this child with homework or on other school-related activities such as reading?

> 0 hrs.   1-2 hrs.   3-5 hrs.   5+ hrs.

207

7. Please indicate who is responding to this survey. (Circle the appropriate choice.)

      FATHER   MOTHER   BOTH

8. How many years have you had a child attending _____? (Include this year and circle the appropriate number.)

      1   2   3   4   5   6   7   8   9   10   10+

Appendix E
Accountability And Accreditation
Getting Involved

OFFICE OF SCHOOL/COMMUNITY RELATIONS

You are encouraged to direct comments or questions to Paul Kemp, Office of School/Community Relations, 635-6113 or 635-6013.

This brochure is available to familiarize the District's citizens with the concept of Accountability and Accreditation and to offer them an opportunity to get involved.

Colorado Springs Public Schools ● El Paso County School District No. 11 ● Dwight M. Davis, Superintendent
Administration Building, 1115 N. El Paso, Colorado Springs, CO 80903-2599

Who Are The Committee Members?

The District's committee is made up of parents, teachers, administrators, non-parent taxpayers, and students.

Each school building has its own committee, too, with the same kinds of representation. Visit your local school to learn about its committee.

District Committee members serve for two years. They are appointed by the Board of Education. If you are interested in serving, contact the Superintendent of Schools, 635-6194.

Meetings are open to the public.

District meetings are held on the third Thursday of each month at 4:00 p.m. at the School District Administration Building, 1115 North El Paso Street.

What Is Accountability?

It's an annual 6-step process for the improvement of schools.

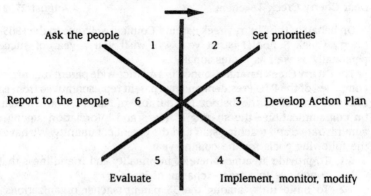

Ask the people   1   2   Set priorities

Report to the people   6   3   Develop Action Plan

Evaluate   5   4   Implement, monitor, modify

What Difference Does It Make?

1. It builds support and confidence in the schools.
2. It improves students' achievement.

Where Did It Come From?

The "Educational Accountability Act of 1971" was enacted by the State Legislature.

Its purposes are:

1. To define and measure quality education.
2. To encourage citizens to help the School Board determine the value of the school program as compared to cost.
3. To measure the adequacy and efficiency of educational programs.

What Is Accreditation?

It's a State law which requires the State Board of Education to accredit school districts. It also requires that all districts be in compliance with the Accountability Act of 1971.

How does a district comply with the Act?

1. The local board must appoint a local advisory committee.
2. The local board must give the committee a charge.
3. The committee must meet, report to the board, and make recommendations.
4. The District must report to the public annually.
5. The District must submit an annual report to the Colorado Department of Education.

209

Appendix F

On behalf of the Cherry Creek Parents' Council, welcome to the 1985-86 Cherry Creek School District year. We wish you a year of success, personally as well as professionally.

The Cherry Creek Parents' Council is a district-wide parent organization composed of the PTO President and two parent representatives from each of the 33 schools in the district. The purpose of Parents' Council centers on communication—the sharing of ideas and information among the administrative and teaching staff and the parent community. We have set the following goals for the coming year:

1. To provide an atmosphere of informality and friendliness that is conducive to a free exchange of ideas.
2. To build unity among the 33 parent/teacher organizations; to extend this unity to teachers, administrators and the Board of Education.
3. To inform the membership of programs and issues within the school district, including the problems of growth, stability, and decline.
4. To give the administrators, Board of Education, and the teachers an opportunity to have direct contact with parent leaders from each school.
5. To keep the membership aware of issues in the county and state that are of interest to Parents' Council and the school district.
6. To provide the opportunity for personal growth.
7. To provide training for all PTO Board members and to encourage participation in all Parents' Council events.

We will accomplish these goals by holding monthly meetings at Smoky Hill High School, offering training workshops for our members, and supporting conferences and special programs throughout the year.

We feel the Cherry Creek School District is unique because of the strong supportive relationship between parents and staff. Parents' Council works cooperatively with the parents, Board of Education, administration, and teachers to maintain a high quality of education for our children. We welcome your support and interest in Parents' Council and look forward to working with you.

Sincerely,
President
Cherry Creek Parents' Council